PUNCHNEEDLE EMBROIDERY

40 FOLK ART  DESIGNS 40

PUNCHNEEDLE EMBROIDERY

40 FOLK ART DESIGNS 40

Barbara Kemp & Margaret Shaw

A LARK/CHAPELLE BOOK

A Division of Sterling Publishing Co., Inc.
New York

A Lark/Chapelle Book

Chapelle, Ltd., Inc.
P.O. Box 9255, Ogden, UT 84409
(801) 621-2777 • (801) 621-2788 Fax
e-mail: chapelle@chapelleltd.com
Web site: www.chapelleltd.com

Editor: Kathy Sheldon
Art Director: Megan Kirby
Cover Designer: Barbara Zaretsky
Illustrator: Orrin Lundgren
Photographer: Steve Mann
Production Assistance: Jeff Hamilton

A NOTE ABOUT SUPPLIERS

Usually, the supplies you need to make the projects in Lark books can be found at your local craft supply store or retail shop relevant to the topic of the book. Occasionally, however, you may need to buy materials or tools from specialty suppliers. In order to provide you with the most up-to-date information, we've created a listing of suppliers on our web site, which we update on a regular basis. Visit us at www.larkbooks.com, click on "Craft Supply Sources," and then click on the relevant topic. You'll find companies listed with their web address and/or mailing address and phone number.

❖ *We wish to thank all the many friends and customers who inspired our efforts and cheered our successes. Barbara gives special thanks to her three children who gave her inspiration to continue forward with her business and this book. Margaret would especially like to thank her family for their loving patience during another "good idea."* ❖

Library of Congress Cataloging-in-Publication Data

Kemp, Barbara, 1953-
  Punchneedle embroidery : 40 folk art designs / Barbara Kemp & Margaret Shaw.— 1st ed.
    p. cm.
  Includes index.
  ISBN 1-57990-889-6 (hardcover)
  1. Embroidery—Patterns. 2. Punched work. I. Shaw, Margaret, 1956- II. Title.
TT771.K42 2006
746.44'041—dc22

                    2006007341

10 9 8 7 6 5 4 3 2 1

First Edition

Published by Lark Books, A Division of Sterling Publishing Co., Inc.
387 Park Avenue South, New York, N.Y. 10016

Text © 2006, Barbara Kemp and Margaret Shaw
Photography © 2006, Lark Books
Illustrations © 2006, Lark Books

Distributed in Canada by Sterling Publishing,
c/o Canadian Manda Group, 165 Dufferin Street
Toronto, Ontario, Canada M6K 3H6

Distributed in the United Kingdom by GMC Distribution Services,
Castle Place, 166 High Street, Lewes, East Sussex, England BN7 1XU

Distributed in Australia by Capricorn Link (Australia) Pty Ltd.,
P.O. Box 704, Windsor, NSW 2756 Australia

Manufactured in China

ISBN 13: 978-1-57990-889-8
ISBN 10: 1-57990-889-6

For information about custom editions, special sales, premium and corporate purchases, please contact Sterling Special Sales Department at 800-805-5489 or specialsales@sterlingpub.com.

❑ CONTENTS ❑

INTRODUCTION

It's an exciting time to be taking up punchneedle. A centuries-old form of embroidery, punchneedle was practiced by ancient Egyptians using the hollow bones of bird wings as needles and by Europeans in the Middle Ages decorating ecclesiastical items and clothing. Brought to the western United States by Russian immigrants, it then took an unfortunate detour into the realm of sad clowns and the avocado greens and burnt oranges of the 1960s and '70s. Now, punchneedle is enjoying a revival, thanks in part to the winning combination you'll find in this book: beautiful hand-dyed flosses and folk art designs.

But the elegant end results—little framable works of art or embellishments for everything from tote bags to journals or chair covers—are only partly responsible for punchneedle's newfound popularity. We've discovered that crafters also love the fact that they can pick up the technique quickly and produce a finished piece in a matter of hours. Punchneedle doesn't require counting stitches or learning complicated techniques—all of our projects use just one stitch, and the same size stitch at that. It's a great craft for our busy times—the needlework is so portable that you can tuck a half-finished piece into a bag and take it anywhere.

So what exactly is punchneedle? Well, the punchneedle tool consists of a hollow handle and hollow needle that strands of embroidery floss (or "thread") flow through. With punchneedle, unlike most embroidery, the design is printed or traced on the back of the fabric being embroidered. The tool is then punched through the back of a hooped piece of fabric in a tiny running stitch to form loops on the front that eventually create a lush, raised design. The weave of the cloth holds the loops in place, so you never even need to tie a knot.

Gorgeous new hand-dyed flosses and simple folk art designs have helped revive the craft of punchneedle.

Punchneedle pieces resemble miniature hooked rugs, and, in fact, rugs are what brought the two of us together. Margaret is a folk art painter and Barbara is a rug-hooker. We met at a national folk art show, and, after chatting a bit, discovered that we live within an

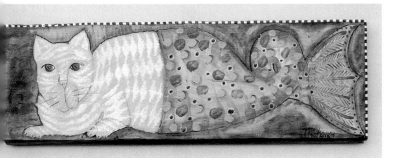

Margaret's folk art paintings, such as the catfish (bottom), serve as inspiration for many of our punchneedle designs (top).

hour of each other in Michigan, both in country homes with cold wood floors. Our first joint project began when we met again the next week to choose and dye wool for the rugs we decided to make together. As our brainstorming and planning continued, a friendship blossomed.

Though in some ways we're different (Margaret has a degree in fine arts, while Barbara's is in accounting), we share a strong independent streak and a devotion to folk art that influences all the designs we've created for this book. We love how each dye lot for the hand-dyed floss is slightly different, how in folk art a bird can be larger than the house it sits on, and imperfection is an advantage.

It wasn't hard to make the leap from rugs to small punchneedle pieces. The gorgeous new flosses available were the perfect match for the folk art designs that Margaret had been painting and Barbara had

been hooking for years. People really responded to this new/old craft that could be accomplished in small snatches of time by all ages at all skill levels, and our punchneedle design business took off.

We're delighted to share our passion for punchneedle with you in these pages. First, in Punchneedle Basics, you'll find the tools and materials you need (not much) and instructions for the techniques you'll use (not difficult). You'll also find directions for finishing projects—tea-staining backing fabrics, framing pieces, or turning them into appliqué patches you can attach to objects. Next, we present step-by-step instructions for 40 projects with templates you can copy from the back of the book. Get started now and you'll have a completed piece in no time. You can reproduce our projects exactly or indulge your own independent streak and experiment. After all, this is folk art.

Barbara designed and hooked rugs (top) for years before trying her hand at punchneedle (bottom).

PUNCHNEEDLE
❋ BASICS ❋

Part of the charm of punchneedle is its simplicity, and this applies, also, to the materials and techniques the craft requires. Everything you need to own to make the projects in this book can fit on a small table or in a small bag. Everything you need to know can be learned in very little time. Let's look first at what you'll need to have.

Handle

Needle

Tools & Materials

BASIC PUNCHNEEDLE SUPPLIES

Punchneedle

Threader

Backing Fabric

Pattern

Floss

Hoop

Sewing Scissors

Embroidery Scissors

Punchneedle. Punchneedles come in a variety of shapes and sizes, but they all consist of a handle attached to a needle with a beveled edge (see figure 1). Both the handle and the needle are hollow—as you punch, the embroidery floss flows through the handle and the needle and then out through the needle's eye. The tool's handle can be made of plastic, wood, or metal; what's important is that you find one that's easy to hold so punching will be comfortable. Some needles are very thin and can accommodate only one strand of floss; some can hold up to six strands. For the projects in this book, you need a needle that can carry three strands of floss.

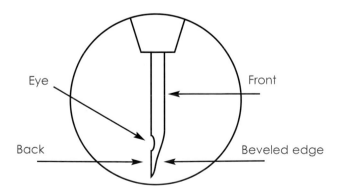

Eye

Front

Back

Beveled edge

The needle depth is important because that's what determines the length of the loops you punch, and thus the look of your finished product. Different effects can be achieved by punching loops of various lengths, but for the folk art projects in this book, you simply set your needle depth at 1/2 inch and leave it there. This results in loops that are all the same length, which contributes to the primitive rug-hooking effect. How you set the needle depth on a particular punchneedle varies from tool to tool— see the manufacturer's instructions.

Threader. A threader is simply a piece of thin wire that's folded in half with a twist in the end. You use it in a two-step process to thread the floss through the punchneedle's hollow handle and needle and then through the needle's eye. (Instructions for using a threader can be found on page 15.) These are marvelously handy tools that unfortunately are so thin they seem to disappear the instant you drop them. Attach a little piece of tape to the unlooped end of your threader, and it will be much easier to keep track of.

Backing Fabric. All of the projects in this book were punched on a backing fabric available at fabric stores or online. It's a polyester/cotton blend that stretches to allow the punchneedle to go through the warp and weft without breaking any of the fibers. This fabric stretches in one direction only; you can figure out the direction of the fabric's stretch by giving it a little tug.

Because the fabric stretches in one direction only as you punch, your finished piece will be slightly longer and narrower than the pattern. The amount of stretch will depend upon your individual style of punching and the amount of floss you punch into the fabric. When you transfer a pattern to a piece of backing fabric, make sure you match the pattern's arrow to the stretch of the fabric; otherwise, your finished piece's dimensions will be distorted.

You can buy backing fabric by the yard and cut it to the size needed. We punched all of the projects in this book on off-white backing fabric, but the cloth is available in a variety of colors.

Patterns. Before you begin punching, you'll need to transfer the pattern to the backing fabric (see page 12 for instructions). When you punch, you're actually working on the back of the fabric (which is facing up in the hoop) as your design is forming on the front of the fabric (which is facing down in the hoop). This means the finished project will be a mirror image of the pattern (see photos on the next page). The patterns in this book are printed actual size, so you don't need to reduce or enlarge them. You can also purchase patterns preprinted on backing fabric, from fabric stores or online.

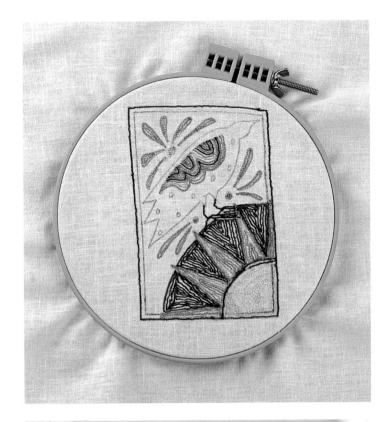

The pattern you punch (top) will be reversed in the finished project (bottom).

Floss. Our folk art pieces are all completed with three strands of six-strand cotton embroidery floss that's available in hand dyed or commercial dyed. If you're new to embroidery you'll be pleasantly surprised at the rainbow of colors available. The hand-dyed floss (sometimes called "overdyed") has subtle color variations that provide automatic shading and movement in your finished pieces. Commercial-dyed floss comes in solid colors that can be used alone, combined with each other, or used in combination with hand-dyed floss. For each of our projects, we've listed the colors we used to create the piece, but feel free to experiment and try different colors. The chart on page 128 can be used to find the color matches for different brands.

Hoop. An embroidery hoop that will hold the fabric tight as a drum is important for proper punching. A 7-inch or larger, no-slip embroidery hoop will work well for most patterns. Old-fashioned tension hoops and wooden hoops won't hold the fabric tight enough.

Sewing scissors and small, sharp embroidery scissors. You'll use the sewing scissors to cut the backing fabric and other fabric used to mat the projects before framing them. The embroidery scissors are for cutting floss ends as close to the backing fabric as possible, so you'll need to find a pair with sharp, thin blades.

Supplies for transferring patterns. The supplies you need to transfer patterns to the backing fabric will depend on which of several possible methods you use. See Transferring Patterns on page 12 for the various methods and the supplies each method requires.

❖ 11 ❖

Getting Ready to Punch

Now that you know the tools and materials you'll need, let's take a look at how you create a punch-needle project.

TRANSFERRING PATTERNS

The patterns can be found starting on page 116. You can use a variety of methods to transfer a pattern to the backing fabric. Experiment with the following to see which works best for you.

Using Transfer Paper. Be sure to use nonsmudging transfer paper if you try this method.

1 Either photocopy the pattern (exact size) or use a pencil to trace the pattern onto tracing paper. If you trace, mark the corners first and then use a ruler to help you trace any straight lines. Be sure to include all design details.

2 Place your backing fabric on a flat surface, set a piece of transfer paper (transfer-side-down) over it, and then place the traced or photocopied pattern over the transfer paper as shown in the photo above. Make sure the stretch of the fabric matches the direction of the arrow on the pattern, and try to place the pattern so lines such as borders are straight on the grain. Tape the pieces so they don't slide around as you're working.

3 Trace the entire pattern with a pen, pressing hard enough to transfer the design onto the fabric. Use a ruler to trace any straight lines, and be sure to include all details. Remove the pattern and transfer paper. You can either use the lines left by the transfer paper or, if you prefer, trace over these lines with a fine permanent marker.

Using a Light Box or a Window. Light boxes can be purchased at craft or camera supply stores. If you don't have one, try this method on a window in daylight.

1 Photocopy the pattern (exact size) or trace it using a writing tool that leaves a dark line. If you trace, mark the corners first and then use a ruler to help you trace any straight lines. Be sure to include all design details.

2 Place the pattern on the light box or tape it to a bright window, and then place the backing fabric over the pattern. If you're using a window, you'll need to tape the fabric in place. Use a fine-point permanent marker to trace the pattern onto the fabric. If you're worried that your hand's not steady enough, trace with a pencil first and then go over the lines with the permanent marker.

Using a Transfer Pen or Pencil. These pens and pencils can be found at craft supply stores.

1 Use a pen or pencil to trace the pattern onto a piece of tracing paper. Mark the corners first and then use a ruler to help you trace any straight lines. Be sure to include all design details.

2 Flip the tracing paper over and, on the back, use a transfer pen or pencil and a ruler to trace over the lines you just drew.

3 Follow the manufacturer's instructions to iron the pattern onto the fabric. Make sure the stretch of the fabric matches the direction of the arrow on the pattern, and try to place the pattern so lines such as borders are straight on the grain. Tape the pieces so they don't slide around as you're working.

BACKING FABRIC'S STRETCH

 Backing fabric stretches in one direction only. When tracing the design to the fabric, make sure arrows on the pattern match the direction of the fabric's stretch (as revealed by a little tug on the fabric); otherwise, the finished piece's dimensions will be distorted.

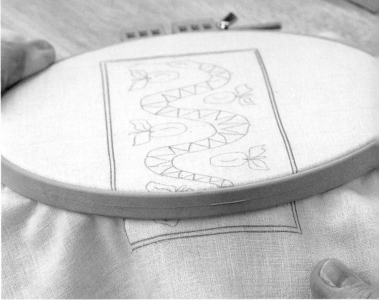

Overhooping

If you're punching a pattern that doesn't fit completely in the hoop, place the fabric so that the left side of the pattern is in the hoop. Once you've punched that side of the pattern, simply remove the hoop, and then enclose the rest of the pattern with it. This technique, called "overhooping," may temporarily crush your punched loops, but they'll spring back—just remove the hoop when you're not working on the project to keep crushing to a minimum.

PLACING THE FABRIC IN THE HOOP

To place the printed backing fabric in a hoop, first loosen the adjustment screw and take the rings apart. Place the fabric, pattern side up, on the inner hoop, and then push the outer ring down over the fabric and the inner hoop. Stretch the fabric so it's very taut as you tighten the outer hoop. (You may have to retighten the fabric from time to time as you're punching the design.)

SEPARATING THE FLOSS

Embroidery floss usually comes with six strands bundled together in a skein. Most skeins consist of one long (8- to 9-yard) length of floss, but some come precut into shorter lengths. Our projects are punched using three strands at a time, so gently separate some of the floss into two three-strand bundles before you begin. The strands should be at least 1 yard long.

Figure 2: Threading a Punchneedle

a. Insert the threader through the hollow needle's tip until the looped end is exposed at the end of the handle.

b. Place floss in the threader's loop.

THREADING THE PUNCHNEEDLE

Threading a punchneedle is a two-step process. You use a wire threader to pull the floss through the punchneedle's handle and needle barrel first; then you use the threader to pull the floss out through the eye of the needle (see figure 2). It looks harder than it is—you just have to try it once or twice and you'll have the hang of it.

c. Pull the threader back out through the punchneedle until about 2 inches of floss are exposed. Gently remove the floss from the threader.

Step 2

a. Insert the threader through the eye of the needle from the back side and again place floss in the wire loop.

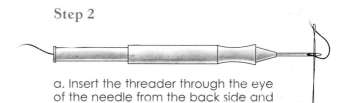

REMOVING FLOSS

To remove floss from the threader, don't tug (or you may break the threader); instead, release the floss from the threader's tiny loop first, then pull on it.

b. Pull the threader and the floss through the needle's eye. Gently remove the floss from the threader.

Punching

Before you begin to punch, make sure the fabric is held taut by the hoop but the pattern isn't distorted from being stretched too much. Hold the hoop so the adjustment screws won't get in the way of the floss as you work.

NEEDLE DEPTH

Follow the manufacturer's instructions to set your needle depth to 1/2 inch. The goal is for your loops to cover the front side of the project without allowing the backing fabric to show through. The 1/2-inch needle depth will provide a short loop that shows details while using the least amount of floss.

TROUBLESHOOTING

If your needle doesn't seem to be punching properly, check the following common problems:

• Make sure the floss is free flowing and not constricted in any way.

• Check to see that the floss is threaded through the eye of the needle.

• Make sure there are no knots in the thread (including in the barrel of the punchneedle).

• Make sure that three threads are threaded through the eye of the needle.

STARTING OFF

The front of the needle is the beveled edge (the part of the needle tip without the eye); this should face the direction you're punching (see figure 3). Opinions differ on how you should hold the punchneedle—we recommend experimenting to find the method that works best for you. What's important is that you try to hold it as vertical as possible; otherwise, it's hard to maintain uniform stitch depths and to avoid catching previously punched loops. About an inch of floss should be coming out of the needle's eye at the back of the needle.

You don't need to knot the floss or overstitch when you begin or end a line of punching. Instead, to begin, simply insert the threaded needle into the fabric and push it through as far as it will go. It's important to punch the needle to the full depth at which it's set with each stitch so the loops that form are all uniform in length.

Raise the needle until the point just pulls through the top of the fabric, drag the tip only a short, fiber-or-two length across the fabric's surface, and immediately punch again. Don't lift the needle off the fabric's surface as this will create an unwanted loop on the back of your project, and keep your stitch length very short. It's not necessary to count threads.

Figure 3: Punching

Top (pattern) side of fabric

Loops forming on bottom side of fabric

Insert the needle into the fabric...

...push it through as far as it will go....

...raise the needle until the point just pulls through the top of the fabric, drag the tip a very short length, and punch again.

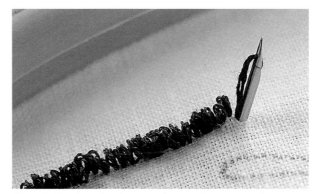

Check the back of your piece often to make sure you're forming neat, uniform loops.

Continue to drag and punch to make a series of small stitches that will, in turn, create a series of loops on the reverse (or front) side of the piece.

Check frequently on the finished side of the piece to confirm that you're creating neat, uniform loops. But don't worry if your punching looks like an unrecognizable jumble of loops initially. Once you punch more of the pattern, the loops will stand taller and the design will emerge. As you get used to the rhythm of the needle sliding just the right length across the fabric, punching, lifting, and then sliding again, you'll soon be able to feel and hear if you're punching correctly.

MINIMIZE JUMPING

Jumping or "traveling" occurs when you cross over an already-punched stitch. It's best to minimize any jumping over punched areas with the needle. Instead, stop, cut the floss, and then begin in the other section even if it's close by. Otherwise, the floss that jumps may block sections that will need to be punched later.

OUTLINING AND FILLING

Outline and fill objects by adding rows of punching. A small amount of space should be left between rows on the side that you're punching, but no fabric should show on the bottom (finished) side of the piece. The closer your stitches are placed together, the farther apart your rows can be.

CUTTING THE FLOSS

When you're ready to stop punching, place your finger on the needle tip to hold the last loop in place, retract the needle, and then use sharp embroidery scissors to clip the floss ends flush with the fabric. No knotting is required. Keep all threads trimmed as you progress.

ORDER OF PUNCHING

You can punch your pattern in any order, but you'll probably find it easiest to punch the border first, the detail next, and the background last. By punching the border first, the perimeter is set, allowing the detail and then background to be outlined and filled. Single-line detail should be punched first when punching the detail portion of a project.

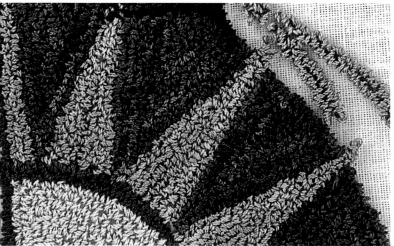

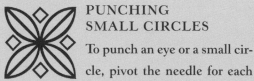

PUNCHING SMALL CIRCLES

To punch an eye or a small circle, pivot the needle for each stitch, making a very tight circle. You can also use just one stitch to make a pupil or eye, but be sure to leave the floss ends slightly longer when you clip them on the back. If you can't see the stitch on the front side, lift the loop carefully with the tip of the needle to achieve the desired look.

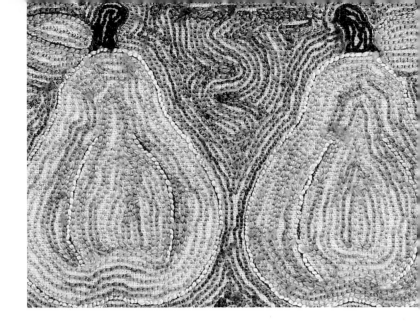

Punch just inside the line when working on the design of any pattern. When you're punching the background, punch just outside the design lines. This will help to keep images in correct proportion—if you punch right on the line for anything except single rows, you'll enlarge the image. Punch around very small details, such as eyes, and complete these last, so they won't get covered by the other loops (see Punching Small Circles on page 18). To create a thin line, punch each stitch slightly farther apart. Punching close together will result in a thicker line.

To form nice tight corners, don't start or finish punching in a corner. When punching an outside corner, punch stitches slightly closer together to define and completely fill out the corner.

REPUNCHING

If you make a mistake (and, let's face it, you probably will at first) or you just aren't happy with the appearance of your loops, you can pull your stitches out and repunch them. Keep in mind, though, that too much pulling may stress the fabric, so try to limit repunching in any one area. Floss can be used again; however, you might need to straighten it first by getting it slightly moist (our high-tech trick is to spit on it). Let it dry before reusing.

FINISHING UP

When all the areas of the pattern are punched, before you take your work out of the hoop, look on the front for any thin spots where the backing fabric shows through. If you see some, punch in additional floss from the back as needed.

Clipping

Clip any floss ends that are showing on the front side. (This happens when the end of the floss exits the needle on a punch and ends up on the front side of the finished piece.)

AMOUNT OF FLOSS NEEDED

It's hard to say just how much of each color of floss you'll need for a project because different skeins hold different yardages, and the amount you use will depend on your punching style. Large areas of color usually require several skeins. For instance, for the pattern One Pair (page 56 and above), we used 20 to 25 yards (four to five skeins) of medium brown for the background and 15 to 20 yards (three to four skeins) of light green gold for the pears and the border. The safest bet is to buy extra floss—we've used many of the same colors in these designs, so you should be able to use any leftovers in another project.

PUNCHING BACKGROUNDS

The technique you use to complete your project's background will contribute to the overall appearance of your piece. You can follow the directions included with each individual design to punch the background, or you can adapt any of the following techniques.

Echoing. This is the basic technique for all backgrounds. With this method, you outline the objects as well as the border with a single color of hand-dyed floss. Continue outlining until there are only small spaces left, and then fill. The color variations within the floss will automatically create color movement. If you're using commercial-dyed floss, thread one color of the floss, and punch. When that floss runs out, thread a color that's close in value, and use that to continue punching, switching back and forth as you use up each color.

Stained Glass. Break the background into geometric shapes and fill with a wide range of colors. This busy background works best when used with a simple object, such as this horse silhouette.

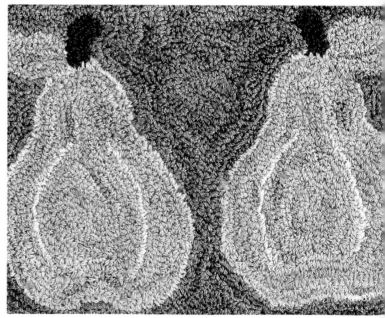

Wiggle and Squiggle. You use two different colors for this method, one darker than the other. Start by punching a wavy line in the darker color in various areas of the background. Add additional rows around the wavy lines in the lighter color, and continue punching rows until the background is complete.

Shadow. Use two colors close in value, such as off-white and cream. Outline everything in the first color. Continue punching in the second color by outlining and filling the background until only a small amount of free space in some of the larger areas remains to be filled. Return to the first color and complete the rest of the background.

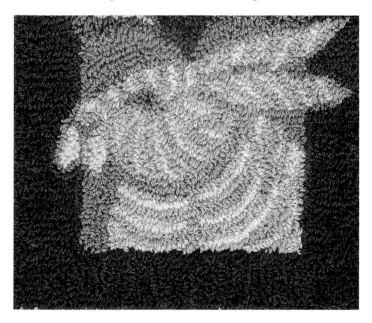

Straight. Straight rows of loops produce the distinct effect you can see in the red "frame" around the rabbit. This method is often used to punch parts of a background rather than the entire thing. The technique is striking when you use a hand-dyed floss in a single color.

Antique. Use a multitude of colors that are close in value. For antique black, select three or four dark values: black, navy, red, and brown, for instance. Using three strands of the same color, outline and fill in small sections, alternating colors as the background is completed. For a light background, use various shades of one color such as white, off-white, and cream. Any color background can be completed with this method as long as the colors in the background are close in value.

Displaying Your Punchneedle

Once you've got your projects punched and pressed, you'll want to show them off to their best advantage. We finished all of the projects in this book in one of four ways:

• We simply framed the piece, using the backing fabric as the mat.

• We antiqued the backing fabric (and sometimes embellished it with embroidery) and then used it as the mat when framing.

• We turned the edges of the backing fabric under and hemmed it, and then used a decorative fabric as a mat when framing.

• We turned the punched piece into an appliqué patch and then attached it to another object, such as a basket or journal.

As you select projects to make in this book, remember that you can follow our example closely or mix and match as you desire. (The size of a piece will change after it's punched. All finishing should be planned around the actual finished size and not the pattern size.) Just about any of these finishing methods will work with any of the patterns. Let's start with the simplest one first.

IRONING

When removing your work from the hoop, the backing fabric will be left with a round wrinkle from the hoop, and your punched area will probably not be as flat as you'd like it. Ironing the piece on the punched and the looped sides with a steam iron should take care of both problems.

SIMPLE FRAMING

One of our favorite ways to display finished punchneedle patterns is with simple framing. You'll probably want to experiment to find the frame that looks best with each piece, but the following steps should work for most frames. This technique, which uses the backing fabric as the mat, comes in especially handy for pieces with scalloped or oddly shaped borders, since those can be difficult to fold over and hem.

WHAT YOU NEED

Punched piece
Frame (with glass is optional)
Craft knife
Scissors
Foam core board
Straight pins
Tape

WHAT YOU DO

1 If your frame came with glass, use it as a guide to cut the piece of foam core board. If your frame doesn't have glass, use the back opening to size your foam core board for cutting. For clean cuts, use the craft knife and cut on one side of the foam core board first; then flip it over and cut the other side.

2 Cut the backing fabric border so it's 2 inches larger on all sides than the foam core board.

Simply framing is an easy yet elegant way to display a punchneedle project.

3 Center the punched piece on the foam core board. Use straight pins to attach the backing fabric to the edges of the foam core board as shown in the photo to the left. Stretch the fabric tight and place the pins about every 1/2 inch until the entire piece is pinned.

4 Fold excess fabric in the back, tape it down, and insert the project into the frame either with or without the glass. (All of the projects in this book were framed without glass.)

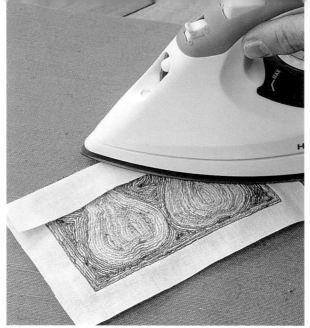

HEMMING AND MATTING WITH A DIFFERENT FABRIC

If you want to use a fabric other than the backing fabric as a mat when framing your punched piece, you'll need to follow the instructions below to hem the edges and hide the backing fabric.

WHAT YOU NEED

Punched piece

Scissors

Iron and ironing board

Double-sided fusible tape

Fabric for matting

Fabric glue (optional)

WHAT YOU DO

1 Cut the backing fabric about 3/4 inch from the edge of the punched area.

2 Place the piece punched-side down on the ironing board. Fold all four sides over and iron so no backing fabric shows on the front of the piece.

3 Place double-sided fusible tape under the folds and iron again to fuse the folds. (Follow the manufacturer's instructions for ironing the fusible tape.)

4 Cut the matting fabric 2 inches larger on all sides than the inside of the frame you'll be using. Then center the hemmed punched piece on the matting fabric, and attach it with fabric glue or double-sided fusible tape and an iron.

5 Follow the directions on page 22 to frame the matted piece.

TEA-STAINING (ANTIQUING) THE BACKING FABRIC

Tea staining is an easy way to give your backing material an antiqued look before framing. You may want to experiment with staining on a scrap piece of backing fabric first to make sure your stain is the shade you prefer. Keep in mind that you can make a light stain darker, but you can't really fix a stain that comes out too dark.

WHAT YOU NEED

Punched piece

Iron

Instant tea or coffee or a tea bag

Hot water

Small stiff-bristle paintbrush

Old towel

Blow dryer (optional)

WHAT YOU DO

1 Iron any hoop wrinkles left in the backing material. If you add tea stain without removing the hoop wrinkle, you'll end up with a darker circle of stain surrounding your project.

2 Mix 1 rounded teaspoon of instant tea or coffee in 1/2 cup of warm water to dissolve the crystals or steep tea bags to get the shade of stain desired.

3 Place your completed punchneedle project on a flat surface (protect the surface from stains first). Use the paintbrush to apply the tea or coffee to the entire exposed backing fabric around the punched design—don't soak the punched area.

4 Place the stained project on the old towel and iron the entire piece dry. Ironing will block the project and minimize any errant loops.

(continued)

5 Place the frame over the piece to judge how the stained background will look when framed. Remove the frame and add more tea or coffee to deepen the stain if you like, or you can add layers of stain for a more distressed effect.

6 Use the blow dryer or iron to finish drying the piece (or allow it to air dry completely) before framing it.

 MAKE SURE YOUR FLOSS IS COLORFAST
Some hand-dyed floss may run when wet; to be safe, test a few strands before punching. If it does run, and you're planning to antique the backing fabric, prerinse the floss before using it to punch the design.

MAKING AN APPLIQUÉ PATCH
Your punched pieces can be used to decorate a variety of objects. Here's an easy way to turn a design into an appliqué patch.

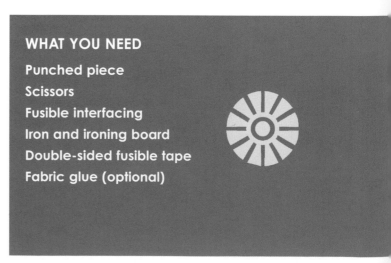

WHAT YOU NEED
Punched piece
Scissors
Fusible interfacing
Iron and ironing board
Double-sided fusible tape
Fabric glue (optional)

WHAT YOU DO

1 Cut the backing fabric about 3/4 inch from the edge of the punched area. Then cut a piece of fusible interfacing that's just a little smaller than the punched area.

2 Set the needlework punched-side-down on the ironing board. Set the interfacing fusible-side-down on the back of the punched area; then follow the manufacturer's instructions to iron it on.

3 Fold all four sides over and iron so no backing fabric shows on the front of the piece. (You may find this easier to do if you miter the corners with cuts first.) Next, place double-sided fusible tape under the folds and iron again to fuse the folds. Follow the manufacturer's instructions for ironing the fusible tape.

 ATTACHING PATCHES
Because appliqué patches are fairly stiff, they can be difficult to sew onto items. It's usually easiest to adhere the patch with double-sided fusible tape. If you're attaching to a hard surface, use a suitable craft glue or hot glue.

4 Your patch is now ready to be attached to the object of your choice. We typically do this by using craft glue or hot glue and a hot-glue gun.

FRAMED PIECES

CHECKERBOARD GAME BOARD

Stylized suns and a scalloped border surround the familiar checkerboard pattern. We chose masculine colors, but you could experiment with a different palette.

PALETTE

Light brown gold

Black

Parchment

Medium gold

Bright gold

Red rust

Burgundy

Slate

Deep brown

PROCESS

1 Punch one line of light brown gold to outline the border, including the scalloped edges.

2 Use black and parchment to punch the checkerboard. To minimize stopping and starting, punch one color of diagonal squares at a time, working from the top to the bottom.

3 Punch the shading for the sun spokes with medium gold and the balance of the spokes with bright gold.

4 Referring to the photos for placement, punch the sun half-circles with red rust and burgundy.

5 To add the background for the suns, punch in straight lines along each ray with slate until the entire wedge shape is filled.

6 Punch the dark decorative line in the border with deep brown.

7 Fill in the remaining border on either side of the deep brown line with light brown gold.

8 For an antique look, you can tea-stain the backing fabric (see page 25), and then stitch random small stars using light brown gold floss before framing.

TOOLS & MATERIALS
Basic punchneedle supplies (page 9)
Pattern (page 118)

FINISHED SIZE: 5 1/4 x 3 inches

BASKET WITH WHITE FLOWERS

This charming little piece is patterned after a painting, right down to the scalloped corners. The design lends itself to various color schemes, so feel free to play with floss choices for both the background and the flowers.

PALETTE

Dark aqua

Off white

Light brown gold

Light apple green

Golden taupe

Dark sage

Parchment

Soft green

Wheat

Dark blue gray

PROCESS

1 Outline the border (except for the basket bottom) with one row of dark aqua.

2 Punch all the basket lines with light brown gold; then fill the remaining area with golden taupe.

3 For the flowers, use parchment, wheat, off white, and golden taupe. Use the photos as guides for color placement. Punch the flower centers with light brown gold.

4 Punch the leaf veins with light apple green. Outline and fill alternating leaves with dark sage and soft green.

5 Punch the background embellishments with dark blue gray. Outline and fill with dark aqua to complete the background.

TOOLS & MATERIALS

Basic punchneedle supplies (page 9)
Pattern (page 122)

FINISHED SIZE: 5 x 4 inches

CROW ON MARINER'S STAR

The first in a series of three projects showcasing that folk art icon the crow, this design incorporates the brush-stroke detailing of the painting on which it was based.

PALETTE

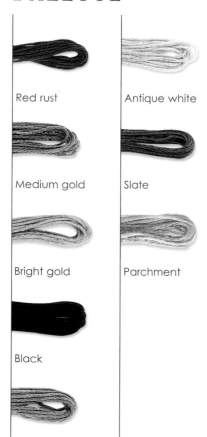

Red rust

Medium gold

Bright gold

Black

Light sage

Antique white

Slate

Parchment

PROCESS

1 Punch one row of red rust to complete the border; then punch the crow's wing lines with red rust.

2 For the wing background, alternate medium gold and bright gold.

3 Outline and fill in the crow's body and feet with black, leaving space for dots and an eye.

4 Complete the dots with light sage. Punch one loop of antique white for the eye.

5 Punch the curved line of the star's center in red rust, tapering to a single line near the bottom. Outline the star spokes and inner sections with medium gold. Fill the remaining star spokes with bright gold.

6 Outline and fill in the wedges between the star spokes with slate. Complete the star center with parchment and antique white.

7 Punch the background embellishments with light sage. Outline the border, crow, and star with parchment; then fill in the balance with antique white.

TOOLS & MATERIALS
Basic punchneedle supplies (page 9)
Pattern (page 125)

FINISHED SIZE: 3 ¹/₂ x 4 ³/₄ inches

CROW ON WATERMELON

Looks like this fellow has found a watermelon and he's ready to crow about it. This piece is one of three projects featuring crows— they work well displayed as a group or separately.

PALETTE

Red rust

Medium gold

Bright gold

Black

Antique white

Dark red

Light sage

Light apple green

Dark sage

Slate

Parchment

PROCESS

1 Punch one line of red rust for the border. Then punch the crow's wing lines in red rust.

2 Fill in the wing background by alternating between medium gold and bright gold.

3 Outline the crow's body and feet in black; then fill the rest of the body with black, leaving a space for the eye. Punch one loop of antique white for the eye.

4 Punch the darker lines on the watermelon flesh with dark red; then fill in the rest of the flesh with red rust, leaving room for the seeds. Punch the seeds with black.

5 Alternate light sage and light apple green to punch the lines on the rind; then fill the remaining area with dark sage as pictured.

6 Outline and fill the checkerboard squares with slate and medium gold.

7 Punch the background embellishments with light sage. Outline the border and the crow with parchment; then fill in the balance with antique white.

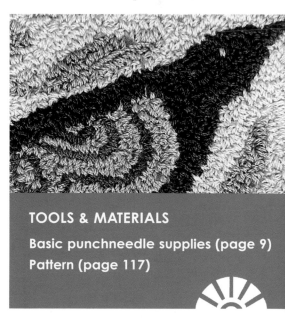

TOOLS & MATERIALS

Basic punchneedle supplies (page 9)
Pattern (page 117)

FINISHED SIZE: 3 1/2 x 5 inches

CROW
ON PINEAPPLE

This time our crow has landed on a pineapple, a symbol of welcome.
While this project fits right in with the other pieces in our crow series,
the scalloped edge adds enough interest for it to stand on its own.

PALETTE

Red rust

Medium gold

Bright gold

Black

Light sage

Antique white

Light brown gold

Dark sage

Parchment

PROCESS

1 Punch a single row of red rust to form the scallop-edged border.

2 Punch the wing lines in red rust; then alternate the wing background with medium gold and bright gold.

3 Outline the crow's body and feet in black; then fill in the body, leaving space for the dots and the eye.

4 Complete the dots with light sage. Punch one loop of antique white for the eye.

5 Punch the pineapple's grid lines with light brown gold; then fill each outer square with medium gold, inner square with bright gold, and center with red rust as shown in the photographs.

6 Using the project photo for reference, punch the leaves with dark sage and light sage.

7 Punch the background embellishments with light sage and red rust. Outline the crow, pineapple, and border with parchment, and fill in the balance with antique white.

TOOLS & MATERIALS

Basic punchneedle supplies (page 9)
Pattern (page 121)

FINISHED SIZE: 3 1/2 x 5 inches

FRUIT BASKET

This piece replicates a painting on an antique plank board table. We gave our fruit basket a dark background, but you could punch a lighter background if you prefer a different look.

PALETTE

Red rust

Golden taupe

Medium green

Dark red

Medium gold

Bright gold

Light green gold

Light brown gold

Dark sage

Black

PROCESS

1 Punch the border (except for the basket bottom) with one row of red rust, followed by one row of medium gold, followed by another row of red rust.

2 Punch the scalloped basket bottom with one row of light brown gold. Outline the rest of the basket with light brown gold. Then fill in the remaining basket area with golden taupe, following the lines on the basket.

3 Punch the pineapple's outline and its interior grid lines using light brown gold. Punch one row of medium gold inside the grid lines, followed by one row of bright gold; then fill in the remaining center area with red rust.

TOOLS & MATERIALS

Basic punchneedle supplies (page 9)
Pattern (page 123)

FINISHED SIZE: 6 1/4 x 4 1/4 inches

4 Punch the pineapple leaves with dark sage and the leaf shading with medium green.

5 Outline and fill the pear and grapes using light green gold. Punch the stems with light brown gold and the grape leaves with dark sage.

6 Punch the green apple with medium green and the red apple with red rust. The stems

and leaves of both apples are punched with dark sage.

7 Punch the strawberries with red rust, leaving space for the seeds. Punch the seeds with black, the leaves with medium green, and the stems with light brown gold.

8 Outline and punch each watermelon section with dark red, leaving space for the seeds,

and then punch the seeds with black. Punch the wavy lines on the rind with light green gold; fill in the remaining area of the rind with dark sage.

9 Outline and fill the background with black.

10 If desired, follow the instructions for tea-staining on page 25 to antique the backing fabric before framing.

SUNFLOWER BASKET

We based this piece on a painting of a stylized sunflower. All the various patterns in the flower, leaves, and basket create interest and movement, while the scalloped black border helps to define the background.

TOOLS & MATERIALS

Basic punchneedle supplies (page 9)
Pattern (page 116)

FINISHED SIZE: 5 x 4 inches

PALETTE

Black

Light brown gold

Golden taupe

Light olive

Dark sage

Red rust

Bright gold

Medium gold

Parchment

Antique white

PROCESS

1 Punch two rows of black for the border. Don't forget to also punch the decorative indents for the border.

2 Punch the basket lines with light brown gold; then outline and fill the rest of the basket with golden taupe. Punch the handles in black.

3 Punch the leaf veins with light olive; then fill the balance of the leaves and the upper leaves with dark sage.

4 Punch the sunflower petals, middle wavy line, and lower lines with red rust.

5 Punch the top and bottom wavy lines and the flower stem in light brown gold. Punch the upper half of the flower in bright gold and the lower half in medium gold.

6 Outline the background with one or two rows of parchment; then fill in the balance of the background with antique white.

CATFISH

You create the strong visual pattern in this piece's background by punching in both straight lines and swirls—we complemented ours with striped matting fabric. You may wish to change the cat's colors to match your own cat.

PALETTE

Black

Red rust

Slate

Bright navy

Bright gold

White

Dark antique gold

Dusty light blue

PROCESS

1 Punch one row of black to form the border.

2 Outline the arms, head, and facial features with black. Fill in the cat's stripes with black; then fill in the balance of the cat's body with slate.

3 Outline the eyes with bright gold; then punch one loop of black for each pupil.

4 Outline the scales with dark antique gold followed by one row of bright gold. Then fill in the center of the scales with red rust. Refer to the photos for proper color placement for the scales.

5 Use bright navy to outline and fill the waves. Then punch the whitecaps with white.

6 Punch the outer water rings with bright navy and the inner rings with dusty light blue, outlining the rings in a contour fashion.

7 Punch straight horizontal lines of dusty light blue to fill the balance of the background.

TOOLS & MATERIALS
Basic punchneedle supplies (page 9)
Pattern (page 118)

FINISHED SIZE: 5 x 3 1/2 inches

SERPENT IN TREE

This design speaks of the biblical Adam and Eve story and also pays tribute to the Shaker tree of life symbol. We think the floss details stitched into the tea-stained backing fabric work well with the distressed frame.

PALETTE

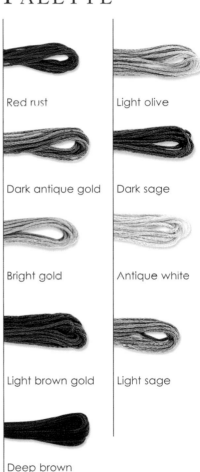

Red rust

Dark antique gold

Bright gold

Light brown gold

Deep brown

Light olive

Dark sage

Antique white

Light sage

PROCESS

1 Punch one row of red rust for the border, making sure to include the notched edges.

2 Outline the snake and its stripes with dark antique gold; then fill in with bright gold, leaving spaces for the red spots on the snake's body. Add one loop of red rust to form each of the spots.

3 Use red rust to punch the tongue and the apples.

4 Punch the lines on the tree with light brown gold; then fill in the remaining tree area with deep brown. Punch a single row of deep brown for each of the two small tree trunks.

5 Use light olive to punch the contour lines on the hill and several leaves (see the photos for placement). Punch the remaining leaves and fill in the hill with dark sage.

6 Outline all objects and the border with antique white. Continue punching rows of antique white until the background is completely filled in.

7 See page 25 for instructions for antiquing the backing fabric. Experiment with stitched embellishments (we used light sage floss) for added charm.

TOOLS & MATERIALS

Basic punchneedle supplies (page 9)
Pattern (page 116)

FINISHED SIZE: 3 1/2 x 5 inches

❖ 45 ❖

RABBIT LOVE

While the irregular top edge of this piece is charming, it's difficult to turn under and hem, so you'll probably want to use the backing fabric as the mat for framing. We added interest by tea-staining the backing fabric and then using floss to embellish it with little stitched sprigs of grass.

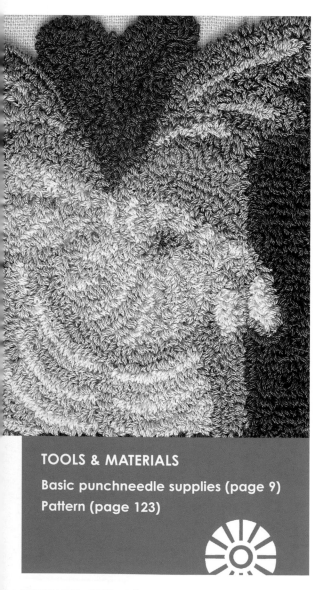

TOOLS & MATERIALS

Basic punchneedle supplies (page 9)
Pattern (page 123)

FINISHED SIZE: 3 1/4 x 3 1/2 inches

PALETTE

Red rust

Light sage

Off white

Parchment

Medium gold

Light apple green

Dark sage

PROCESS

1 Ignoring the heart and leaves for now, use red rust to punch one row to set the outside border and one row to set the inside border. Fill in the border by punching straight lines parallel to these rows you just punched. Use the dotted lines on the pattern to help you create "mitered" corners, which make the border look like a frame.

2 Outline and then fill in the heart with red rust.

3 Outline the rabbit's face and body with light sage; then punch the rabbit's cheeks and the lines on the rabbit with off white. Use parchment to punch the remainder of the rabbit.

4 Fill in the background with medium gold.

5 Punch the insides of the leaves with light apple green and the outer parts of the leaves with dark sage.

6 Follow the directions on page 25 to tea-stain the backing fabric. Once the fabric is completely dry, you can use a single strand of dark sage floss to hand-stitch little grass sprigs.

HIGHRIDER BICYCLE

This simple, elegant picture of a bygone era will enhance any traditional décor. Using hand-dyed floss and the echoing technique to fill the background make it appear that the bike is in motion.

PROCESS

1 Punch several rows of dark rust to form the outer border. Add one row of slate for the inner border.

2 Punch a single line of slate to form the bicycle; fill in with slate for the seat, the handle, and the pedals.

3 Outline and fill all objects with medium gray until the background is completely filled in.

4 If you choose to hem the finished piece and mat it with a decorative fabric, follow the directions on page 24.

TOOLS & MATERIALS
Basic punchneedle supplies (page 9)
Pattern (page 122)

FINISHED SIZE: 6 1/4 x 4 1/4 **inches**

PALETTE

Dark rust

Slate

Medium gray

SQUIRREL

This piece looks like a miniature hooked rug. It's adorable framed or as a rug in a dollhouse. The subtle variations in the background add movement to the piece.

PALETTE

Dark antique gold

Dark red brown

Dark sage

Deep brown

Light sage

Antique white

Medium brown

Parchment

PROCESS

1 Punch the border in dark antique gold. You can also punch the branch and the nut part of the acorns at this time with dark antique gold.

2 Outline the leaves with dark sage; then fill with light sage.

3 Punch some of the acorn caps with medium brown and some with dark red brown (use the photos for reference).

4 Use deep brown to punch the lines and eye on the squirrel. Then use medium brown to complete the remainder of the squirrel.

5 Begin filling the background by outlining all objects with antique white. Continue to outline, randomly mixing antique white and parchment, until the entire background is filled.

6 Follow the instructions on page 24 to hem the finished piece and mat it with decorative fabric before framing. If you're going to use the finished piece as a rug in a dollhouse, follow the instructions on page 26 to turn it into an appliqué patch.

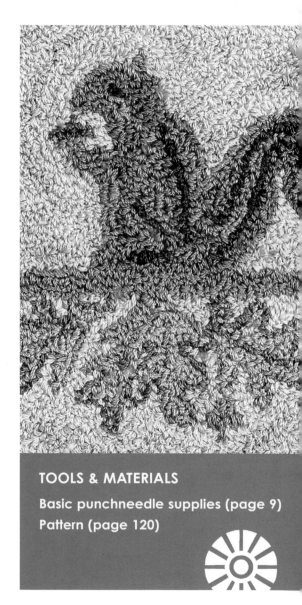

TOOLS & MATERIALS

Basic punchneedle supplies (page 9)
Pattern (page 120)

FINISHED SIZE: 5 1/4 x 3 1/4 inches

❖ 51 ❖

FRAKTUR BIRD

This design was inspired by Pennsylvania Dutch pen-and-watercolor Fraktur art and then stylized in the Margaret Shaw tradition. We antiqued the backing fabric and found a green frame that complements the needlework colors nicely.

PALETTE

Black

Red rust

Light brown gold

Deep brown

Medium gold

Bright gold

Golden taupe

Dark sage

Parchment

Antique white

PROCESS

1 Outline the border with a single row of black.

2 Punch the wing, the tail, and the inner flowers with red rust, leaving room on the wing and the tail for the details in light brown gold.

3 Punch the lines on the tail, the embellishment on the wing, the inner petals of the flowers, and the six lower spots on the bird with light brown gold.

4 Use deep brown to punch the bird's head, the upper spots on the bird, and the flower stems. Punch the feet, the beak, and the center of the eye with black.

5 Punch the bird's body and outline the outer flower petals with medium gold. Fill in the centers of the outer petals with bright gold.

6 Punch the wavy lines for the ground with light brown gold and fill in between with golden taupe.

7 Outline and fill the leaves with dark sage (the color variations you can see in the photos will occur naturally if you use hand-dyed floss).

8 Outline the bird, the flowers, and the ground with parchment. Fill in the balance of the background with antique white.

9 You can tea-stain the backing fabric, if you like, by following the instructions on page 25.

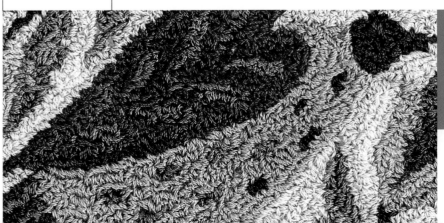

TOOLS & MATERIALS
Basic punchneedle supplies (page 9)
Pattern (page 117)

FINISHED SIZE: 5 x 3 1/4 inches

STAINED-GLASS HORSE

The background behind this horse silhouette gives the effect of a stained-glass window if you use colors with similar values. Keep this project in mind when you have odds and ends of leftover floss to use up.

PALETTE

Black

A wide variety of colors of your choice

PROCESS

1 Punch three rows of black to form the border.

2 Outline and fill the horse with black.

3 Outline and fill each background section with a color of your choice.

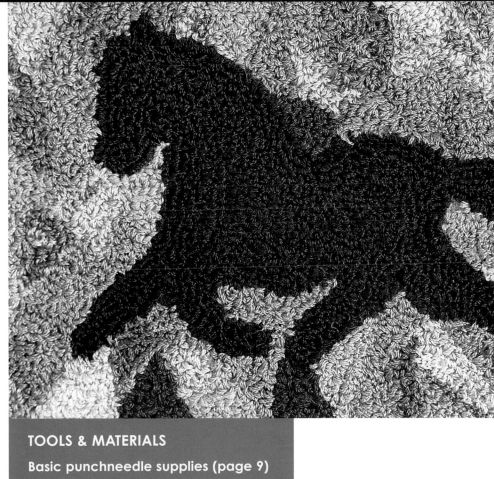

TOOLS & MATERIALS
Basic punchneedle supplies (page 9)
Pattern (page 119)

FINISHED SIZE: 5 1/2 x 3 1/2 inches

ONE PAIR

Punch these perfect mirror images in subtle color variations to create a simple, elegant picture. We've displayed ours with a flax-colored linen mat and a wood frame, but a bright mat and frame could be used instead for a different effect.

PALETTE

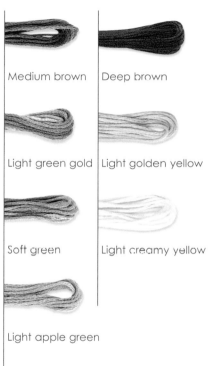

Medium brown

Deep brown

Light green gold

Light golden yellow

Soft green

Light creamy yellow

Light apple green

PROCESS

1 Outline the border with one row of medium brown and then one row of light green gold, to create a simple border.

2 Outline the leaves and veins with soft green, then fill with light apple green. Then punch the stems with deep brown.

3 Outline the pears in light golden yellow; then punch the highlights on the pears in light creamy yellow. Outline and fill in the balance of each pear with light green gold.

4 Fill in the background by outlining the pears and border with medium brown until the background is complete. Using this echoing technique and hand-dyed floss will create the interesting background.

5 If you choose to hem the finished piece and mat it with a decorative fabric, follow the directions on page 24.

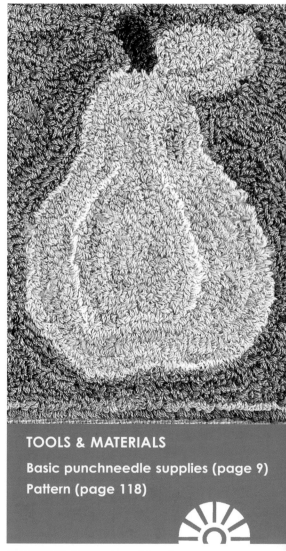

TOOLS & MATERIALS
Basic punchneedle supplies (page 9)
Pattern (page 118)

FINISHED SIZE: 6 x 4 inches

SOME PIG

This lone pig bordered by a wattle fence makes a whimsical little hanging.
If you think he needs some friends, punch two more pigs
in different colors for a complete set of three.

PALETTE

Light apple green

Medium peach

Black

Dark blue gray

Dark peach

PROCESS

1 Punch the wattle fence border with light apple green. Then outline and fill the outer border with black.

2 Punch one row of light apple green for the inner border.

3 Outline the pig, the leg lines, and the tail with dark peach.

4 Outline and fill in the balance of the pig with medium peach, leaving space for the eye. Punch the pig's eye with black.

5 Outline the pig and the border with dark blue gray. Continue to outline and fill in the background until it's completely filled in.

TOOLS & MATERIALS

Basic punchneedle supplies (page 9)
Pattern (page 127)

FINISHED SIZE: 5 1/2 x 4 inches

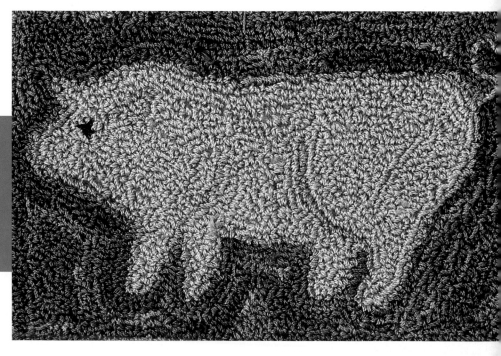

STARS

*Here's a simple star design that can be adapted to many different color schemes.
You won't be able to punch perfect stars, and that's a good thing—
their asymmetrical shapes give the piece its quaint look.*

PALETTE

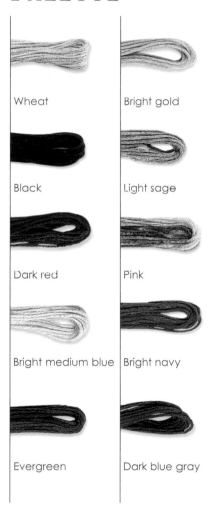

Wheat

Black

Dark red

Bright medium blue

Evergreen

Bright gold

Light sage

Pink

Bright navy

Dark blue gray

PROCESS

1 Outline the border with a row of wheat to set the perimeter.

2 Outline the large center star with two rows of black. Outline each smaller star with one row of black.

3 Fill in the large center star with dark red; then, using the photos for color placement, fill two of the small stars with bright medium blue, two with evergreen, two with bright gold, two with light sage, two with pink, two with bright navy, and two with dark blue gray. (You may also use your own choice of colors to create an individual look.)

4 Outline all stars and the border with wheat until the background is completely filled in.

5 If you choose to hem the finished piece and mat it with a decorative fabric, follow the directions on page 24.

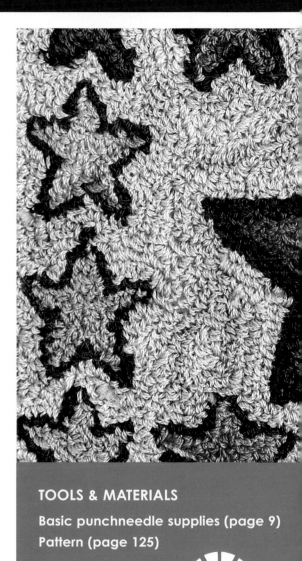

TOOLS & MATERIALS
Basic punchneedle supplies (page 9)
Pattern (page 125)

FINISHED SIZE: 4 1/2 x 3 1/4 inches

LOG CABIN GEOMETRIC

This project is based on the traditional log cabin design, often seen in quilts and rug hooking. Because what you're punching on the back of the fabric is always the reverse of the finished piece, getting the colors in the right place can be a little tricky with this one, but the results are well worth the effort.

PALETTE

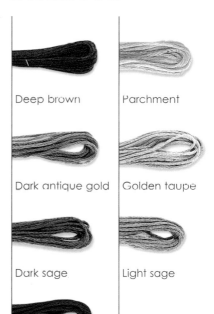

Deep brown

Parchment

Dark antique gold

Golden taupe

Dark sage

Light sage

Dark red

PROCESS

1 Punch two or three rows of deep brown to set border.

2 Fill all the center squares with deep brown.

3 You create this piece's design by using dark and light color values. Notice on the pattern (page 120) that each of the 15 large squares is divided into a longer and a shorter side. The longer sections are always completed with the dark values (dark antique gold, dark sage, and dark red), and the shorter sections are always completed in the lighter colors (parchment, golden taupe and light sage). Keep this in mind when placing the colors, especially when working in reverse on the back of the piece. The pattern will emerge as the punching progresses.

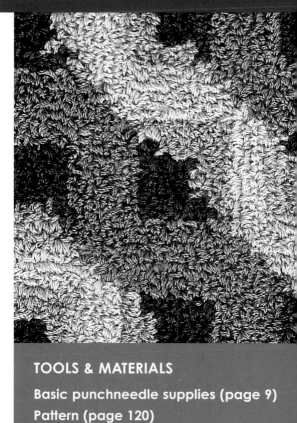

TOOLS & MATERIALS

Basic punchneedle supplies (page 9)
Pattern (page 120)

FINISHED SIZE: 5 1/2 x 3 1/4 inches

GEOMETRIC SQUARES

This pattern is based on traditional rug-hooking and quilt designs. It's perfect framed, or you could instead turn the finished piece into a patch and use it as a rug in a dollhouse.

PALETTE

Black

Slate

Dark sage

Dusty light blue

Light olive

PROCESS

1 Outline the border by punching several rows of black.

2 Punch a single row of black for the grid.

3 You create the pattern in this piece by using the darkest color values on the larger, outer squares and the lightest color values in the center squares. Start with slate on the outside, progress to dark sage, dusty light blue, and then light olive in the center. Feel free to substitute different colors—just use the same method for placing colors values.

4 If you decide to frame the finished piece and mat it with a decorative fabric, follow the directions on page 24. If you're going to use the finished piece as a rug in a dollhouse, follow the directions for making an appliqué patch on page 26.

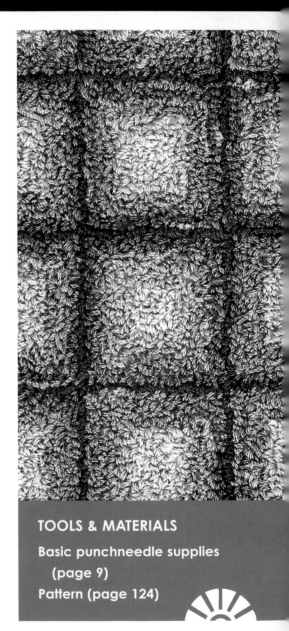

TOOLS & MATERIALS

Basic punchneedle supplies
   (page 9)
Pattern (page 124)

FINISHED SIZE: 3 1/4 x 5 1/2 inches

HONEYCOMB GEOMETRIC

A simple geometric using just a few colors can create this intricate design.
The contrasting calico print we used as a mat really helps this piece stand out.

PALETTE

Black

Dark red

Antique white

Dark blue gray

Bright gold

PROCESS

1 Punch two rows of black for the border.

2 Punch the grid lines (see the pattern on page 124) with a single row of black.

3 Outlines the grid lines using dark red, then antique white, and then dark blue gray.

4 Fill in the centers with two rows of bright gold.

5 If you choose to hem the finished piece and mat it with a decorative fabric, follow the directions on page 24.

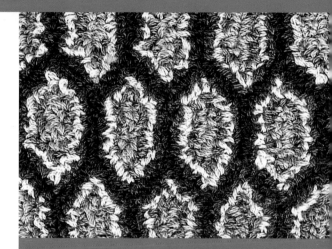

TOOLS & MATERIALS

Basic punchneedle supplies (page 9)
Pattern (page 124)

FINISHED SIZE: 2 1/2 x 5 inches

BETSY ROSS FLAG

This flag with 13 stars in a circle and 13 stripes will make a great addition to your patriotic collection. The muted colors and dark antiqued border give the piece the look of a treasured heirloom.

PALETTE

Dark antique gold

Charcoal blue

Wheat

Dark red

PROCESS

1 Set the border by punching three rows of dark antique gold.

2 Punch the stars with wheat; don't worry about trying to form perfect stars.

3 Fill in the field behind the stars with charcoal blue.

4 Complete the stripes on the flag by alternating dark red and wheat (each stripe will probably require three rows of punching).

5 Follow the instructions on page 25 to antique the backing material. We used coffee instead of tea to give ours an extra dark stain to add to the aged appearance of the project.

TOOLS & MATERIALS

Basic punchneedle supplies (page 9)
Pattern (page 127)

FINISHED SIZE: 5 x 3 1/4 inches

WELCOME
PINEAPPLE

This welcoming piece makes a nice housewarming gift or addition to any home. You create the design's interesting background by using as many dark colors as possible to outline the pineapple.

PALETTE

Red rust

Dark antique gold

Medium gold

Bright gold

Dark sage

Various dark colors

PROCESS

1 Punch three rows of red rust to set the border.

2 Outline the pineapple and punch the grid lines with a row of dark antique gold followed by one row of medium gold.

3 Fill in the balance of the pineapple sections with bright gold, leaving enough room to punch two loops of dark sage in the center of each.

4 Use dark sage to punch the foliage on the top and bottom of the pineapple.

5 Punch the letters with red rust. Keep in mind that the letters will be reversed as you punch, but they'll be correct on the finished side.

6 Create the background by outlining the pineapple and foliage with various dark colors of floss until the background is completely filled in.

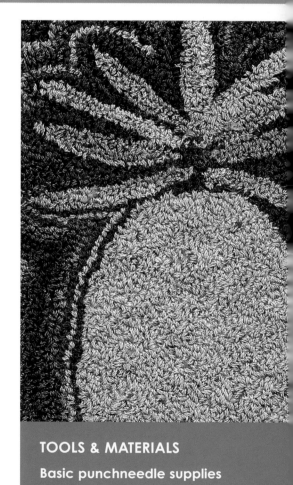

TOOLS & MATERIALS

Basic punchneedle supplies (page 9)
Pattern (page 125)

FINISHED SIZE: 5 1/2 x 4 inches

HOME

The border framing our charming cottage was punched in straight rows using a variety of dark colors. We matted our piece with a quilted backing fabric to add to the homey effect.

PALETTE

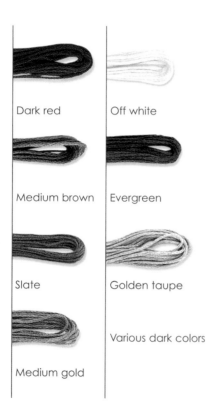

Dark red

Off white

Medium brown

Evergreen

Slate

Golden taupe

Various dark colors

Medium gold

PROCESS

1 To make the border, first punch the letters for HOME in dark red. Keep in mind that the letters will be reversed as you punch, but they'll be correct on the finished side. Then punch the border using a variety of dark colors in straight lines. Alternate the colors to create an interesting border. Add a row of dark red on the inside of the border.

2 Make the fence by punching one row of medium brown; then fill in the path and the chimney with same color.

3 Punch the roof and the line down the front corner of the house with slate. Punch the line across the side of the house with medium brown.

4 Punch the door and the shutters with dark red, leaving room to punch the windows with medium gold.

5 Outline and fill the remainder of house with off white.

6 Outline and fill the trees with evergreen.

7 Complete the background by outlining all objects and the border with golden taupe. Continue to outline until the background is completely filled.

8 If you choose to hem the finished piece and mat it with a decorative fabric, follow the directions on page 24.

TOOLS & MATERIALS

Basic punchneedle supplies (page 9)
Pattern (page 126)

FINISHED SIZE: 5 1/4 x 3 1/4 inches

STAR GAME BOARD

This is the first in a series of three small, square game boards.
These pieces look terrific as a group or individually.

PALETTE

Black

Golden taupe

Dark red

Medium gold

Bright navy

Antique white

Slate

PROCESS

1 Punch one row of black to set the border.

2 Punch a single row of black to form all the grid lines of the game board.

3 Outline and fill in the stars using the photos for color placement. If you want the colors to be placed in a certain order, keep in mind as you punch that the design on the finished side will be the reverse of what you're punching.

4 Complete the game board grid with the star colors (golden taupe, dark red, medium gold, and bright navy) and antique white, again using the photos for color placement. Remember to leave room for the black playing pieces.

5 Use black to make the game board's playing pieces.

6 Fill in the corner backgrounds behind the stars with slate to complete the project.

7 To antique the backing fabric before framing the finished piece, follow the instructions on page 25.

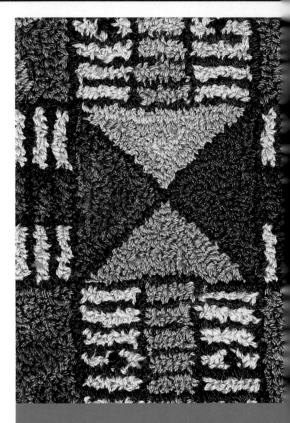

TOOLS & MATERIALS
Basic punchneedle supplies
(page 9)
Pattern (page 127)

FINISHED SIZE: 4 x 4 inches

MAN IN THE MOON GAME BOARD

This, the second in a series of three small, square game boards, features a cheerful moon surrounded by four suns.

PALETTE

Slate

Bright gold

Evergreen

Dark blue gray

Dark red

Dusty light blue

Off white

Golden taupe

Black

PROCESS

1 Set the border by punching one row of slate. Then punch all the gridlines with a single row of slate.

2 Punch all suns in bright gold; then fill in their centers with slate.

3 Punch the backgrounds behind the suns in evergreen, dark blue gray, dark red, and dusty light blue. Punch the centerlines in the grids in the same colors, leaving room for the black playing pieces.

4 Punch the moon's eye, eyebrow, and cheek details with slate. Use dark red to punch the lips and off white for the teeth.

5 Fill in the moon and the outer rows of the gridlines with golden taupe. Then fill in the background behind the moon with dark blue gray.

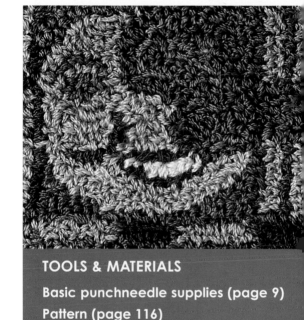

TOOLS & MATERIALS

Basic punchneedle supplies (page 9)
Pattern (page 116)

FINISHED SIZE: 4 x 4 inches

6 Add several loops of black to form the game board's playing pieces.

7 To antique the backing fabric before framing the finished piece, follow the instructions on page 25.

COMPASS GAME BOARD

This, the third in a series of three small, square game board projects, plays with colors and features a compass design.

PALETTE

Black   Evergreen   Medium rust   Bright navy   Dark red   Golden taupe

PROCESS

1 Punch one row of black to form the border.

2 Make the grid lines by punching a single row of black.

3 Using evergreen, medium rust, bright navy, and dark red, punch two rows to outline each of the four outer circles. Punch the compasses and small inner circles in the same colors, remembering to leave room inside the small circles to add black dots.

4 Using the photos for color placement, punch the multi-colored circle, compass, and small circles in the center of the game board.

5 Use evergreen, medium rust, bright navy, and dark red to punch the centerlines in the grids, using the project photo for color placement and leaving room for the black playing pieces.

6 Punch a loop of black inside each small circle, and then use black to make the game board's playing pieces.

7 Fill in the backgrounds behind the compasses with golden taupe.

TOOLS & MATERIALS
Basic punchneedle supplies (page 9)
Pattern (page 123)

FINISHED SIZE: 4 x 4 inches

WEARABLES & HOME ACCENTS

TWO PATRIOTIC BARRETTES

Turn these patriotic punchneedle pieces into wearable art by attaching them to barrettes (or even items such as jeans or jackets). You don't need to stick with our traditional color scheme—unexpected colors can give you playful results.

PALETTE

Red rust

Charcoal blue

Wheat

Dark red

Golden taupe

PROCESS

For the four-star barrette:

1 Punch one row of red rust for the border.

2 Outline and fill the second star from the left with wheat. Outline and fill the other three stars with golden taupe. (If you're using different colors, you can achieve the same effect by punching one star in a lighter color value than the rest.

3 Outline the border and the stars with charcoal blue. Continue outlining and filling with charcoal blue until the background is completely covered.

4 Follow the instructions on page 26 to turn the finished piece into an appliqué patch. Then use the hot glue and hot-glue gun or craft glue to attach the patch to the barrette.

For the flag barrette:

1 Punch the star with golden taupe; then fill in the background behind the star with charcoal blue.

2 Punch two straight lines for each stripe, alternating dark red and golden taupe as shown in the photo.

3 Follow the instructions on page 26 to turn the finished piece into an appliqué patch. Then use the hot glue and hot-glue gun or craft glue to attach the patch to the barrette.

TOOLS & MATERIALS
Basic punchneedle supplies (page 9)
Patterns (pages 126 and 127)
2 barrettes, 3 1/2 x 1 inches
Hot glue and hot-glue gun
  or craft glue

FINISHED SIZE (EACH): 4 x 1 inches

WATERMELON CHICKEN CHALKBOARD

This charming piece was the perfect embellishment for a chalkboard made from a piece of a salvaged door. You could use a patch made from this pattern to decorate all manner of kitchen items, or simply frame your needlework and hang it in any spot that needs a little summer cheer.

PALETTE

Black

Parchment

Light apple green

Light blue

Red rust

Antique white

Dark sage

Dusty light blue

Dark antique gold

Burgundy

Light brown gold

Dark blue gray

Medium gold

TOOLS & MATERIALS

Basic punchneedle supplies (page 9)
Pattern (page 126)
Salvaged wood door
    panel or other piece of wood
Sandpaper or hand sander
Scroll saw (optional)
White latex or acrylic paint
Paintbrush
Painter's (or masking) tape
Chalkboard paint
Saw-tooth picture hanger
Craft glue

FINISHED SIZE: 4 1/2 x 3 1/4 inches

PROCESS

1 Outline the border with a single row of black.

2 Punch the wing lines using red rust and dark antique gold; then fill in the balance of the wing with medium gold.

3 Use parchment to outline the chicken; then fill in the balance with antique white, leaving spaces for the circles.

4 Outline three circles in dark antique gold; then finish all the circles on the chicken with black. Punch the chicken's feet in black. Punch the comb and wattle in burgundy.

5 Punch the watermelon flesh with red rust, leaving spaces for the seeds; then punch the seeds with black. Punch the rind's curvy lines in dark antique gold and the wavy lines in light apple green. Then fill in the remaining rind with dark sage.

6 Use light apple green to punch the seedlings on the ground and light brown gold to fill in the remaining ground.

7 Punch the upper and lower sky with light blue, the sky's upper center with dusty light blue, and its lower center with dark blue gray to create the cloud-like effect.

8 Follow the instructions on page 26 to turn the finished piece into an appliqué patch.

9 Clean the salvaged door panel or other piece of wood (if necessary), and then sand it. Make the V-shaped cuts with the scroll saw and then sand the edges to taper the cuts.

10 Paint the entire front with white latex or acrylic paint, and let it dry completely. Sand the edges, allowing previous layers of paint to show for distressed look.

11 Mark off the section for the chalkboard with masking tape. Then paint this area with the chalkboard paint (this section was raised on our salvaged door). After the paint has dried completely, remove the tape and sand the edges to distress.

12 Attach a saw-tooth picture hanger on the back.

13 Use the craft glue to adhere the patch to the top of the chalkboard.

PENNSYLVANIA FLOWERS BASKET

This floral pattern borrows from the Pennsylvania Dutch heritage with its flowers and small heart at the base of the design. It seemed perfect for our rust-colored basket. Create the design's interesting background by using the echoing technique to outline and fill with colors of similar value.

PALETTE

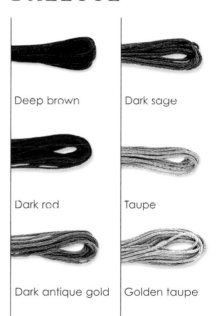

Deep brown

Dark sage

Dark red

Taupe

Dark antique gold

Golden taupe

Dusty pink

PROCESS

1 Spray-paint the basket if desired. Allow it to dry completely.

2 Punch two rows of deep brown to create the elongated hexagonal border.

3 Punch the center of the outer flowers with dark red, and then outline each with one row of dark antique gold. Using the photos for reference, punch the body and the petals of these outer flowers with dusty pink; then punch their inner petals with dark red.

4 Use dusty pink to punch the outside petals of the large tulip in the center; then punch

(continued)

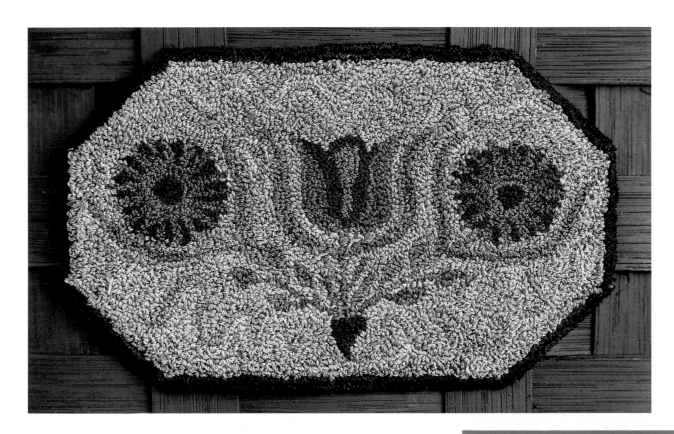

the inner petals with dark red. Use dark antique gold to fill the tulip center.

5 Punch all the leaves and the stems with dark sage.

6 Use dark red to punch the heart.

7 Punch the wavy lines in the pattern's background with taupe. Outline the deep brown border with one row of taupe.

8 Fill in the background by outlining the wavy taupe lines and all other elements with golden taupe. Finish the background by filling in any small spaces.

9 When you've finished punching, follow the directions on page 26 to turn the punched piece into an appliqué patch.

10 Use hot glue and the hot-glue gun to attach the patch to the basket. You can use a hair dryer to heat the basket to help thin out the wax glue and create a good bond. To do so, heat the basket where the patch will be applied, and run beads of hot wax in an area at least 1/4 inch smaller than the size of the patch. Press the patch onto the hot glue and hold it in place until the glue cools. Let up pressure if glue starts to seep out from the edges.

TOOLS & MATERIALS

Basic punchneedle supplies (page 9)
Pattern (page 117)
Basket
Spray paint in coordinating color (optional)
Hair dryer (optional)
Hot glue and hot-glue gun

FINISHED SIZE: 5 1/2 x 3 1/2 inches

SIX STARS BOOK EMBELLISHMENT

*Depending on the color scheme you choose, this pattern can be used
to enhance all manner of objects (the finished piece also looks great simply framed).
If you're interested in altered books, follow our lead and use it to embellish a cover.*

PALETTE

Red rust

Bright gold

Antique white

Medium gold

Light sage

Black

Parchment

Light brown gold

Slate

PROCESS

1 Punch the border, including the scallops, in red rust. Use the same color to punch the two small diamond-shaped background embellishments.

2 Punch all of the stars points, referring to the photo for color placement. Keep in mind that the finished result will be the reverse image of the side you're punching.

3 Outline each large circle. Notice that we gave some of these large circles an outer rim of another color.

4 Punch the innermost star circles and then the circle surrounding each.

5 Punch the wedge-shaped backgrounds behind the star points.

TOOLS & MATERIALS

Basic punchneedle supplies (page 9)
Pattern (page 121)
Craft glue
Old book

FINISHED SIZE: 3 1/2 x 4 1/2 inches

6 Complete the background by outlining and filling around the circles and the scalloped border with light brown gold.

7 To use the finished needlework to decorate a book cover, follow the instructions on page 26 to turn the piece into an appliqué patch.

8 If you are altering the inside of the book, do so before attaching the appliqué patch to the cover. Adhere the appliqué patch to the cover with craft glue.

HEART FLORAL KEEPSAKE BOX

This project makes a lovely gift for a wedding or other special event. Just change the date on the pattern to suit your purposes (or you can leave the date off altogether). If you change the date, just remember to reverse the numerals on the pattern so they'll be correct on the finished side.

PALETTE

Wheat

Light olive

Dusty pink

Charcoal blue

Dark sage

Burgundy

Dusty light blue

Parchment

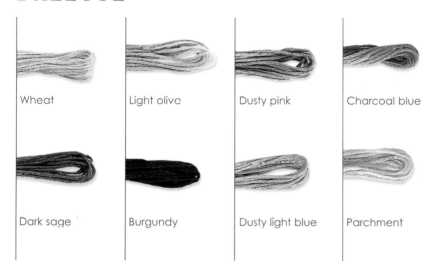

PROCESS

1 If you're going to finish the box with paint or stain, do so now so it will be completely dry before you attach the punch-needle heart.

2 Punch one row of wheat to set the border.

3 Punch the stems and leaf veins on the lower leaves with dark sage. Use light olive to outline and fill the leaves.

4 Punch the date in the small heart with one row of burgundy. Keep in mind that the numbers will be reversed as you

(continued)

TOOLS & MATERIALS

Basic punchneedle supplies (page 9)
Pattern (page 119)
Wooden box
Craft glue

FINISHED SIZE: 6 ¼ x 3 ¼ inches

punch, but they'll be correct on the finished side. Use dusty pink to fill in the small heart, leaving spaces for the dots. Punch the dots on the heart with burgundy.

5 Using the photos as reference for color placement, outline and fill the flowers with dusty light blue and dusty pink, leaving spaces for the dots on the dusty light blue flowers.

6 Referring to the photos again for color placement, complete the flowers with burgundy and charcoal blue.

7 Punch the wavy lines in the background using the darker color value of wheat. (These subtle lines are hard to see in the photos, but clearly marked on the pattern.)

8 Use parchment to fill the background by outlining the wavy lines, the border, and all other elements. This will create interesting detail in the background of the project. Finish the background by filling in any small spaces with parchment.

9 When you're done punching the piece, follow the instructions on page 26 to turn the punched piece into a patch.

10 Use the craft glue to adhere the patch to the lid of the wooden box.

APPLE SERPENT EYEGLASS CASE

Do you have a hard time keeping track of your reading glasses? Have you heard the phrase "if it were a snake, it would bite you"? Our folk art serpent is certainly eye-catching—we've never known a snake to get so many compliments.

PALETTE

Black

Burgundy

Red rust

Light apple green

Bright gold

Dark sage

Medium gold

Parchment

Light sage

PROCESS

1 Begin the punchneedle piece by outlining the border with a single row of black and then a single row of red rust.

2 Referring to the photos for color placement, punch the alternating triangles on the snake's body with red rust, bright gold, and medium gold.

3 Punch the snake's head with bright gold, leaving a space for the eye. Then punch the eye with light sage and a single loop of black for the pupil.

4 Punch the tongue with a single line of red rust. Use red rust to punch the apples, adding one small line of burgundy to create shading.

(continued)

5 Alternate leaves with light apple green and dark sage as pictured; each light apple green leaf gets a vein of dark sage.

6 Outline the snake, the border, and all apples with light sage; then fill in the remainder of the background with parchment.

7 Follow the instructions on page 26 to turn the finished piece into an appliqué patch.

8 Cut a piece of double-sided fusible interfacing just slightly smaller than the punched patch. Place first the interfacing and then the patch on the front of the eyeglass case and iron to bond.

TOOLS & MATERIALS
Basic punchneedle supplies (page 9)
Pattern (page 120)
Soft eyeglass case
Double-sided fusible interfacing
Iron

FINISHED SIZE: 6 1/4 x 2 3/4 inches

WHITE CAT JOURNAL

*This is one of our smaller folk art punchneedle pieces. It makes a delightful
little framed work, but it also can be turned into an appliqué patch
and then made into a pin or used, as we've done here, to embellish a journal cover.*

PALETTE

Red rust

Dark sage

Light sage

Antique white

Parchment

Black

Light apple green

Soft green

Dark red

PROCESS

1 Outline the top section of the border with one row of red rust and the bottom section of the border with dark sage.

2 Outline the cat and its facial features with light sage. Punch the cat's nose and cheeks with antique white and then randomly fill the rest of the face and the body with antique white and parchment (use the photos to help you with color placement).

3 Punch the eyes with dark sage and a single loop of black for the pupils.

4 Fill in the background with light apple green and soft green. Punch three loops of dark red to form each irregular dot on the background.

5 Follow the instructions on page 26 to turn the finished piece into an appliqué patch. Then attach the patch to the journal cover with the hot glue and hot-glue gun.

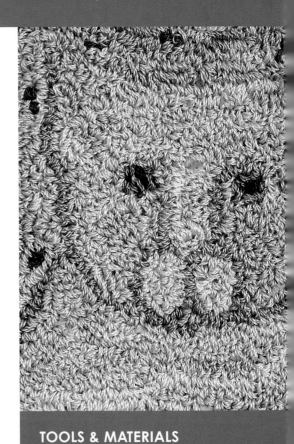

TOOLS & MATERIALS

Basic punchneedle supplies
  (page 9)
Pattern (page 121)
Hot glue and hot-glue gun
Journal

FINISHED SIZE: 2 1/2 x 2 1/2 inches

PUNCHNEEDLE PROJECT BASKET

This cheerful basket lets you keep your projects-in-progress close at hand.
We purchased this basket secondhand and spray-painted it rust red,
but you can use any basket large enough to hold a hoop and other supplies.
Make two patches if you'd like to attach one to each side of your basket.

PALETTE

Black

Burgundy

Red rust

Dark sage

Bright gold

Parchment

Medium gold

Wheat

PROCESS

1 Spray-paint the basket if desired. Allow to dry completely.

2 Outline the border with one row of black.

3 Punch the shading on the left edges of the flowers petals with burgundy; then fill the rest of each petal with red rust. Punch the leaves and stems with dark sage.

4 Outline the outer circle of each dot in the flower with bright gold and then add a ring of red rust inside that. Use parchment next, and then punch the center of each dot with black. Use medium gold to fill the inside of the flower.

(continued)

TOOLS & MATERIALS

Basic punchneedle supplies (page 9)
Pattern (page 118)
Basket with a handle
Spray paint in coordinating
color (optional)
Hair dryer (optional)
Hot glue and hot-glue gun

FINISHED SIZE: 2 1/4 x 2 1/2 inches

5 Outline the flower and border with wheat. Continue to outline and fill until the entire background is filled.

6 Follow the instructions on page 26 to turn the finished piece into an appliqué patch.

7 Use hot glue and the hot-glue gun to attach the patch to the basket. You can use a hair dryer to heat the basket to help thin out the wax glue and create a good bond. To do so, heat the basket where the patch will be applied, run beads of hot wax in an area at least 1/4 inch smaller than the size of the patch. Press the patch onto the hot glue and hold it in place until the glue cools. Let up pressure if glue starts to seep out from the edges.

OLIVE HENS CHAIR COVER

This whimsical chair cover will cheer up any kitchen and is simple to make. The punchneedle piece is attached to the backing fabric with iron-on double-sided fusible tape. The fabric is sewn onto the dishtowel chair cover with a running stitch that's both decorative and allows you to remove the fabric so you can wash the cover.

PALETTE

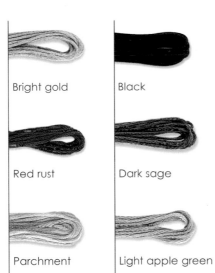

Bright gold

Black

Red rust

Dark sage

Parchment

Light apple green

Light sage

PROCESS

1 To punch the pattern's irregular border, first outline the entire border with one row of bright gold; then punch each successive row by working from the outside in and tapering off, using the pattern and photos for reference.

2 Punch the hens' wing lines, combs, and wattles in red rust. Punch the remainder of the wings with bright gold.

3 Use parchment to outline and fill each hen, leaving space for the decorative circles.

4 On the hen with its head down, punch the outer circles with one row of light sage; then fill the inner circles with black and add one loop of parchment. For the hen with its head up, punch the outer circles with two rows of light sage, and use red rust for the centers.

(continued)

TOOLS & MATERIALS

Basic punchneedle supplies (page 9)
Pattern (page 121)
Swatch of contrasting fabric, 6 3/4 x 4 3/4 inches
Ruler or measuring tape
Double-sided fusible tape
Iron
Dishtowel (ours was 20 x 28 inches)
Thread in a contrasting color
Sewing needle
4 large buttons that coordinate with fabric and towel

FINISHED SIZE: 5 1/4 x 3 1/4 inches

5 Punch the feet and legs with single rows of black. Then use dark sage to punch the seedlings in the background. Fill in the remaining background with light apple green.

6 Follow the instructions on page 26 to turn the finished punchneedle piece into an appliqué patch.

7 Fold the edges of the coordinating fabric under ³/4 inch on all sides and set the hem with double-sided fusible tape, following the manufacturer's instructions.

8 Place the dishtowel over the back of the chair it will be covering to determine the best placement for the punchneedle patch and its fabric mat.

9 Hand-stitch the fabric mat to the front of the dishtowel, using a large running stitch approximately ¹/4 inch from the edge.

10 Secure the punchneedle patch to the backing fabric with double-sided fusible tape.

11 Sew the four buttons on the bottom corners.

milk
eggs
juice

WATERMELON MAGNETS

These cheerful watermelon magnets will allow you to turn any metal surface into a memo board. If you've already got a fridge-worth of magnets, you could instead use these slices of summer to embellish a jacket or a kitchen item.

PALETTE

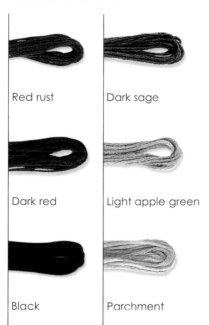

Red rust

Dark sage

Dark red

Light apple green

Black

Parchment

PROCESS

1 Outline and fill the red area on the wedge-shaped slice with red rust, leaving the spaces for the seeds. Outline and fill the red area on the half watermelon with dark red, again leaving the spaces for the seeds.

2 Punch the seeds with black.

3 Punch the wavy lines on the rinds with dark sage alternating with light apple green and parchment (use the photos for color placement). Fill in the remaining rind with dark sage.

4 Follow the instructions on page 26 to turn the finished piece into an appliqué patch.

5 Place each patch onto the adhesive side of the magnet sheet, trace around the shapes with the pen or pencil, and then cut the shapes out with scissors.

6 Adhere the magnets to the backs of the patches.

TOOLS & MATERIALS

Basic punchneedle supplies
   (page 9)
Patterns (pages 116 and 122)
Adhesive-backed magnet sheet
Pen or pencil
Scissors

FINISHED SIZES:

HALF-WATERMELON: 3 x 2 inches

SLICE: 3 x 1 ¹/₂ inches

TWO
PATRIOTIC PINS

The subtle hues of hand-dyed floss give these pins their antique look—they go with our patriotic barrettes on page 80. Use patches made from the punched pieces to embellish clothing or other items, as well, and feel free to play with the color palette.

PALETTE

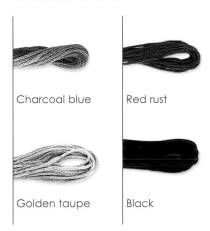

Charcoal blue

Red rust

Golden taupe

Black

PROCESS

For the four-star pin:

1 Set the border and grid with one row of charcoal blue.

2 Punch the stars by outlining and filling with golden taupe. Fill the background behind the stars with red rust.

3 Follow the instructions on page 26 to turn the finished piece into an appliqué patch.

Then cut out a piece of felt, just slightly smaller than the patch, and attach it to the patch with the hot glue and hot-glue gun or craft glue.

4 Use the hot glue and hot-glue gun or craft glue to secure the pin back to the patch.

For the flag pin:

1 Punch the border with one row of black.

2 Use golden taupe to punch the star. Then fill in the field behind the star with charcoal blue.

3 Punch two or three straight rows for each stripe, alternating red rust and golden taupe as shown in the photos.

4 Follow the instructions on page 26 to turn the finished piece into an appliqué patch. Then cut out a piece of felt, just

slightly smaller than the patch, and attach it to the patch with the hot glue and hot-glue gun or craft glue.

5 Use the hot glue and hot-glue gun or craft glue to secure the pin back to the patch.

TOOLS & MATERIALS

Basic punchneedle supplies (page 9)
Patterns (pages 117 and 124)
Scrap of wool or felt, 4 x 4 inches
1- to 1 1/2-inch-long pin backs (available online and at craft stores)
Hot glue and hot-glue gun or craft glue

FINISHED SIZE:
FOUR-STARS: 2 x 1 1/2 inches
FLAG: 2 1/2 x 1 3/4 inches

SWAYING SUNFLOWER BAG

Hand-dyed floss works with color and line to create the movement you can almost feel in this design. Small silk bags can be found at craft shops or online. This piece also looks lovely framed.

PALETTE

Black

Burgundy

Red rust

Dark antique gold

Bright gold

Deep brown

Light apple green

Soft green

Parchment

PROCESS

1 Punch one row of black for the border.

2 Referring to the photo for placement, punch the shadow lines and the centers of the petals with burgundy.

3 Punch the remainder of all petals and the wavy lines with red rust.

4 Punch the detail at the bottom of the large sunflower with dark antique gold; then fill in the balance of both flowers with bright gold.

5 Punch a single row of deep brown to form each stem.

6 Punch the center of the leaves with light apple green; then outline and fill the balance of the leaves with soft green.

7 Punch the background embellishment with dark antique gold.

8 Outline all objects and the border with parchment, and then fill in the remaining background with parchment.

9 Follow the instructions on page 26 to turn the finished piece into an appliqué patch.

10 Cut a piece of the double-sided fusible interfacing just slightly smaller than the patch. Place first this and then the patch on the front of the bag, and iron to bond the patch to the bag.

TOOLS & MATERIALS

Basic punchneedle supplies (page 9)
Pattern (page 124)
Purchased silk bag in complementary color
Double-sided fusible interfacing
Iron

FINISHED SIZE: 4 x 5 inches

RABBIT AND STARS BOOK BAG

It's nice to use your punchneedle on items you can take out into the world. This bag is a cinch to make—it's just a placemat with two sides stitched up and handles attached. The punchneedle patch was bonded with easy double-sided fusible interfacing. You could use the same method to attach this, or any of our other designs, to a purchased bag.

PALETTE

Black

Light sage

Antique white

Parchment

Bright gold

Medium gold

Red rust

Slate

Light brown gold

PROCESS

1 Begin the punchneedle piece by punching a single line of black to set the border.

2 Outline the rabbit in light sage. Punch the lines on the rabbit in antique white; then fill the rabbit's body in with parchment. Use bright gold to punch the rabbit's eye.

3 Follow the color placement in the photos to punch the stars and their circles.

4 Punch the sun flares with red rust. Punch the sun centers with bright gold, and then use slate to fill the wedges between the sun flares.

5 Outline all objects and the border with light brown gold until the background is filled.

6 Follow the instructions on page 26 to turn the finished punchneedle piece into an appliqué patch. Set the patch aside for now.

7 It's easiest to attach the strap handles before sewing up the bag. If you're making straps from fabric, fold both long edges on each strip over 1/2 inch, and iron. Fold each strip again, this time in half, folded sides together, and pin. Topstitch each strip 1/8 inch in along one edge, turn and stitch the bottom edge, and then stitch back up the

(continued)

TOOLS & MATERIALS

Basic punchneedle supplies
(page 9)
Pattern (page 119)
Two 36 x 2-inch fabric scraps,
or 2 yards of 1/2-inch webbing
Iron
Straight pins
Sewing machine
Fabric placemat
(ours was 19 x 14 inches)
Double-sided fusible interfacing

FINISHED SIZE: 6 1/4 x 3 inches

opposite edge, again 1/8 inch in. If you're using webbing, simply cut it into two 36-inch lengths.

8 To attach the handles, first lay the placemat right side up. Fold one end of one strap under about 3/4 inch and topstitch it to one short edge of the placemat, forming an X to reinforce the stitching. (As you can see in the project photo on page 111, our handles were attached to the outside of the bag, about 4 inches in from on each side.) Be careful not to twist the strap as you're attaching it. Repeat to attach the other end of the same strap. Then repeat this same procedure with the other strap on the opposite end of the placemat.

9 Fold the placemat, right sides together, and sew up the sides. To box the bottom of the bag, flatten out one side seam and pull the corners of the bag out from each side of the seam to form a triangle. Measure and sew a 3-inch line perpendicular to the side seam, about 1 1/2 inches down from the point. Repeat on the other side. Turn the bag right side out.

10 To attach the punchneedle patch to the front of the bag, cut double-sided fusible interfacing just slightly smaller than the patch. Set the interfacing and then the patch in place on the front of the bag, and iron to bond the patch.

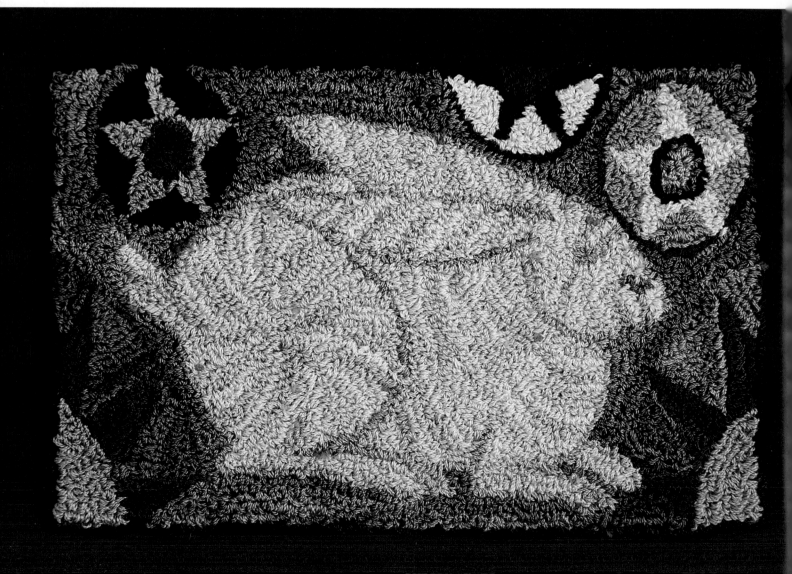

PENNSYLVANIA DUTCH LIDDED BASKET

This sweet pattern is the perfect example of how punchneedle can turn something as simple as a purchased basket into an heirloom. This design works well with the other pieces that share its Pennsylvania Dutch influence, on pages 85 and 90.

PALETTE

Light brown gold

Dusty pink

Charcoal blue

Dark red

Dusty light blue

Golden taupe

Dark sage

Parchment

PROCESS

1 Punch several rows of light brown gold to set the border.

2 Referring to the photos for color placement, punch the inside lines and petals on the large outer flowers with charcoal blue. Punch the outer and center petals in dusty light blue. For the small flowers inside the heart, punch the inner petals with charcoal blue and the outer petals with dusty light blue.

3 Use dark sage to punch all the leaves and stems.

4 Outline and fill the heart and the lines on the heart with dusty pink. Fill in the balance of the heart with dark red.

5 Punch the wavy lines in the background with light brown gold.

6 Alternate between golden taupe and parchment to fill the background by outlining the wavy lines, the border, and all other elements.

7 Follow the instructions on page 26 to turn the completed piece into an appliqué patch.

8 Use the hot glue and the hot-glue gun to attach the patch to the lid of the basket.

TOOLS & MATERIALS

Basic punchneedle supplies (page 9)
Pattern (page 126)
Basket with lid
Hot glue and hot-glue gun

FINISHED SIZE: 5 1/2 x 3 1/2 inches

PATTERNS

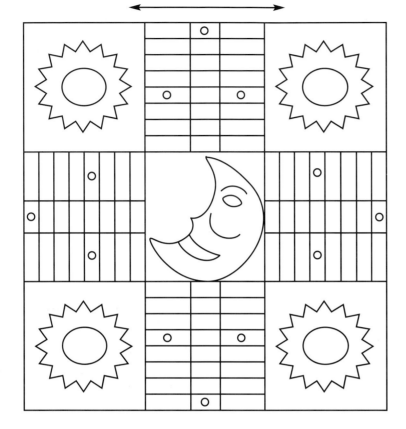

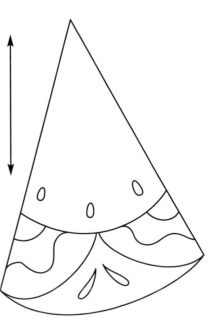

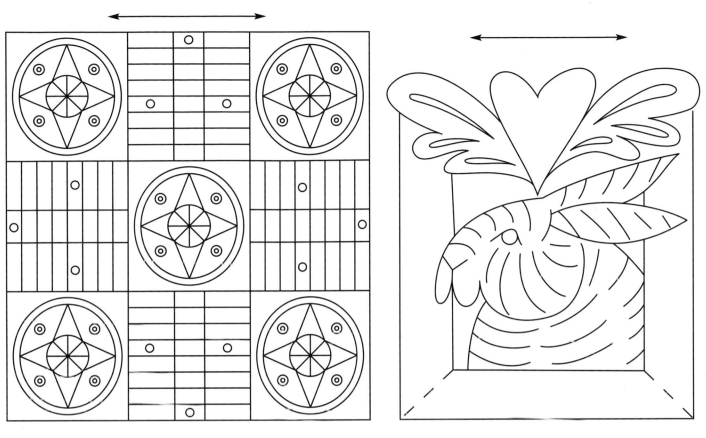

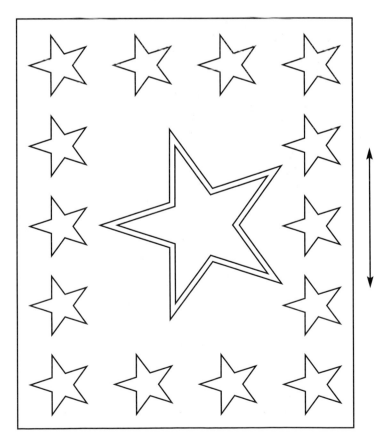

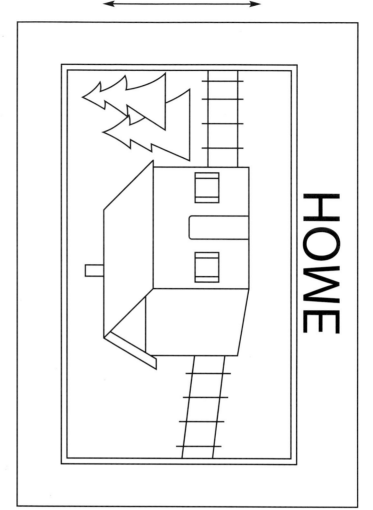

HOME

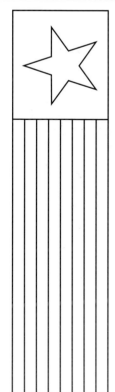

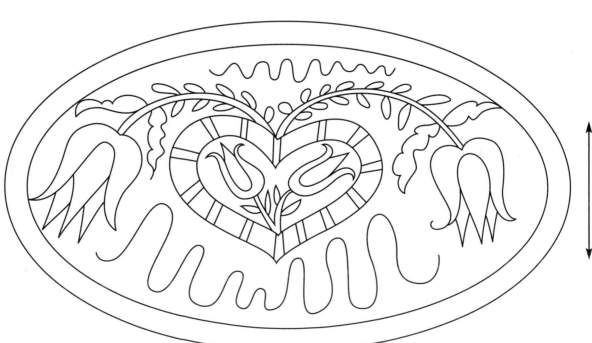

(Use this chart as a general guide to color names. Hand-dyed flosses vary greatly between dye lots, so inspect colors before purchasing.)

HAND-DYED FLOSS COLOR NAMES

Generic Names	Gentle Art	Weeks Dye Works
Antique White	Shaker White	Beige
Black	Black Crow	Mascara
Bright Gold	Gold Leaf	Whiskey
Bright Medium Blue	Cornflower	Sky
Bright Navy	Midnight	Deep Sea
Burgundy	Cherry Bark	Crimson
Charcoal Blue	Tin Bucket	Dolphin
Dark Antique Gold	Tarnished Gold	Chestnut
Dark Aqua	Peacock	Teal Frost
Dark Blue Gray	Brethren Blue	Twilight
Dark Peach	Cider Mill Brown	Cinnabar
Dark Red	Cranberry	Lancaster Red
Dark Red Brown	Walnut	Mocha
Dark Rust	Sarsaparilla	Hazelnut
Dark Sage	Dried Thyme	Bark
Deep Brown	Dark Chocolate	Molasses
Dusty Light Blue	Old Blue Paint	Dolphin
Dusty Pink	Antique Rose	Raspberry
Evergreen	Blue Spruce	Juniper
Golden Taupe	Harvest Basket	Oak
Light Apple Green	Green Apple	Kudzu
Light Blue	Morning Glory	Dove
Light Brown Gold	Maple Syrup	Havanna
Light Creamy Yellow	Buttermilk	Buttercup
Light Golden Yellow	Summer Meadow	Honeysuckle
Light Green Gold	Cornhusk	Daffodil
Light Olive	Grasshopper	Olive
Light Sage	Chamomile	Scuppernog
Medium Brown	Sable	Mocha
Medium Gold	Grecian Gold	Schneckley
Medium Gray	Banker's Grey	Pewter
Medium Green	Shutter Green	Bayberry
Medium Peach	Adobe	Conch
Medium Rust	Nutmeg	Terra Cotta
Off White	Oatmeal	Whitewash
Pink	Clover	Camelia
Parchment	Parchment	Taupe
Red Rust	Mulberry	Brick
Slate	Soot	Gun Metal
Soft Green	Grape Leaf	Seaweed
Taupe	Wood Smoke	Cocoa
Wheat	Flax	Fawn
White	Picket Fence	Whitewash

METRICS CONVERSION CHART

INCHES	METRIC (MM/CM)	INCHES	METRIC (MM/CM)	INCHES	METRIC (MM/CM)	INCHES	METRIC (MM/CM)
$1/8$	3 mm	2	5 cm	$9^1/2$	24.1 cm	17	43.2 cm
$3/16$	5 mm	$2^1/2$	6.4 cm	10	25.4 cm	$17^1/2$	44.5 cm
$1/4$	6 mm	3	7.6 cm	$10^1/2$	26.7 cm	18	45.7 cm
$5/16$	8 mm	$3^1/2$	8.9 cm	11	27.9 cm	$18^1/2$	47 cm
$3/8$	9.5 mm	4	10.2 cm	$11^1/2$	29.2 cm	19	48.3 cm
$7/16$	1.1 cm	$4^1/2$	11.4 cm	12	30.5 cm	$19^1/2$	49.5 cm
$1/2$	1.3 cm	5	12.7 cm	$12^1/2$	31.8 cm	20	50.8 cm
$9/16$	1.4 cm	$5^1/2$	14 cm	13	33 cm	$20^1/2$	52 cm
$5/8$	1.6 cm	6	15.2 cm	$13^1/2$	34.3 cm	21	53.3 cm
$11/16$	1.7 cm	$6^1/2$	16.5 cm	14	35.6 cm	$21^1/2$	54.6 cm
$3/4$	1.9 cm	7	17.8 cm	$14^1/2$	36.8 cm	22	55 cm
$13/16$	2.1 cm	$7^1/2$	19 cm	15	38.1 cm	$22^1/2$	57.2 cm
$7/8$	2.2 cm	8	20.3 cm	$15^1/2$	39.4 cm	23	58.4 cm
$15/16$	2.4 cm	$8^1/2$	21.6 cm	16	40.6 cm	$23^1/2$	59.7 cm
1	2.5 cm	9	22.9 cm	$16^1/2$	41.9 cm	24	61 cm
$1^1/2$	3.8 cm						

ACKNOWLEDGMENTS

The following companies contributed supplies for this book:

Hooked-on-Rugs
Mason, MI
www.punchneedlepatterns.com

The Gentle Art
New Albany, Ohio
www.thegentleart.com

Eastside Mouldings
Lititz, Pennsylvania
www.eastsidemouldings.com

Weeks Dye Works
Garner, North Carolina
www.weeksdyeworks.com